TRIUMPHS OF THE FOOTBALL FIELD

TRIUMPHS OF THE FOOTBALL FIELD

NARRATED BY

ARCHIE HUNTER

(THE FAMOUS VILLA CAPTAIN)

First Published in Great Britain in by the Birmingham Weekly Mercury (1890)
Re-published in Great Britain in 1997 by
SPORTS PROJECTS LTD
188 Lightwoods Hill, Smethwick, Warley, West Midlands B67 5EH

•

ISBN 0 946866 44 9

•

•

A catalogue record for this book is available from the British Library

•

Design and layout by Sports Projects Ltd

•

Printed by Polar Print Group Ltd

Contents

Chapter 1

Leather Hunting: Past and Present

The simple fact that I, the chronicler of these 'Triumphs', have never attended a football match in my life; that I have always ignored those spirited and graphic reports which have now become at once my delight and my despair; that such terms as 'half-back', 'forward', 'dribbling' and 'off-side' have always been as mysterious in their import as the hieroglyphics on an Egyptian pyramid – should be deemed a sufficient and special qualification for the task I have set myself to perform.

Even I, however, in my outcast state, had heard of Archie Hunter, and in some dim way had discovered that he was a hero of the Football Field and the gallant leader in many a famous victory. Time was when the rousing cry of "Play up, Villa", burst from ten thousand throats and when the anxious eyes of a vast unnumbered multitude watched the lithe form of Archie as he passed the leather, or when with irresistible energy and scientific tact he delivered a shot for goal. It is not so long ago since excited and enthusiastic crowds thronged the streets and rendered the public thoroughfares almost impassable in order to meet the conquering hero on his return from a decisive match and follow him with acclamations long and loud to his home.

For ten years he was the idol of the sport-loving public. He was admired for his redoubtable powers, his dash and skill on the field, his true sportsmanlike behaviour and his unvarying good-temper and fairness towards his opponents. He believed in a true exposition of the game and in winning by merit; and though the temptations to 'rough' the other side are often strong, no one forbore more than Archie Hunter to take other than a legitimate advantage in the struggle for victory.

With a quick eye for the weak spot in the opposing team, ready in resource and able to put forth tremendous strength, which his knowledge of the game enabled him to use judiciously, Hunter not only achieved many brilliant exploits himself, but was a source of inspiration and encouragement to those whom he led. He played to win, and played his best and the result was that the Villa team grew in power and reputation, until finally the greatest of all honours signalised their supremacy over all competitors.

This result was, of course, long in its attainment and in these articles it is proposed to narrate, in Archie Hunter's own words, all the important and memorable events which led up to it, and to relate what he and his comrades did to obtain it. In the course of the narrative many familiar names will be introduced and many a battle will be fought again. But the story of noted victories told by the Villa captain will be invested with new interest and made vivid with personal details which have never been supplied before; and therefore the 'twice-told tale' cannot be dull or tedious.

It is scarcely necessary to state, at the outset, that the game of football dates back to times of the greatest antiquity. It may have come over with the Conqueror, like many another noble thing boasting the claims of long descent. Or, more likely, it was a pastime of the hardy old Saxons who fought so well to maintain their own, and who doubtless had some knowledge and experience of heavy 'charging' and 'hacking'. But football, like the human species, has always been going through a number of evolutionary changes and it is rather difficult to trace the resemblance between the football of today and the football of the remote past.

It is true that in each case there was a ball, and that the ball was kicked; likewise that there were men to kick it. But here the parallel ceases. Even the stately old Greeks and Romans were not averse to footing the leather, and it must have been a sublime spectacle to behold the wise men of Rome and Athens throwing off the toga, donning the 'jersey' and displaying their skill in dribbling or covering themselves with glory in a scrimmage.

Imagination could conjure up many a lively scene when these

veterans of old times engaged in a match and when the grave and reverend citizens assembled in the thousands to see the kick-off at 2.30 on a Saturday afternoon. But unfortunately, Archie Hunter remembers nothing of these things, so whether on these occasions Rugby or Association was played must remain an open question.

The history of football in this happy land is decidedly peculiar. Centuries ago the young Britons played the game with so much vigour that the pastime had all the dangers of a pitched battle and it led to so many broken limbs and wounded pates that the public peace was disturbed, and numerous attempts were made to prohibit the sport by legal restrictions. But what cared young England for law and order where their favourite sport was concerned? Dislocated shoulders and bruised legs could not restrain their ardour, was it to be expected that the threat of a fine or of a day in the stocks would be effectual? Certainly not.

So football continued to be played, although in the reign of King Edward II all 'hustling over large balls' was sternly forbidden; while in King Edward III's reign a vigorous attempt was made to abolish the game altogether.

It is the proud boast of Englishmen that they like something to 'knock about', and it is a common belief that if they did not do this with cricket and football they would in sheer despair employ their fists and feet in 'knocking about' each other. It is therefore not at all surprising to find that when football declined prize-fighting became the rage, and that when the latter noble sport began to sink in popular estimation football again came to the fore. It was not the stringent laws of Elizabeth that suppressed football for a time; they had but little effect. But Puritanism succeeded in doing that which the laws for centuries had failed to do; and had it not been for the public schools there can be little doubt that after Cromwell's time football would have become as much a thing of the past as the Olympian sports.

On Shrove Tuesday, however, all England was wont to awaken to the fact that football was still a national pastime, and with goals several miles apart they would chase the leather across country from sunrise until sunset. Nor has this Shrove Tuesday footballing yet been entirely discontinued. A correspondent of the Field gave the following curious account of the custom as it prevailed so late as 1888:-

"At Ashbourne, in Derbyshire, the inhabitants appeared to be in an excited state on Shrove Tuesday. I naturally inquired the cause and was told there was to be a football match in the afternoon. It surprised me not a little to find so much interest taken in a game of football by all classes, from the doctor to the labourer. Whilst at lunch I learnt the cause of this intense excitement. It appears that it is a very ancient custom to play a game of football every Shrove Tuesday; it is long looked forward to, and much party feeling is displayed.

The rules of the game in question are rather curious ones. In the first place the number on each side is unlimited. There is a bridge in the centre of the town, and everybody living north of this is on one side and everybody living south of the bridge is on the other side (no matter whether one lives 20 yards north of it or in John-O'-Groats, or for the matter of that in the Shetland Isles). The goals are three miles apart and consist in two mills, each one about one and a half miles from the town. Before a goal can be claimed, not only does the ball have to touch the mill, but the player has to swim across the millpond and touch the building himself. Any player securing the goal in the manner described gets 10s. and considering the amount of hard work, that there were several inches of snow on the ground, and that the temperature had been below freezing point all day, the final plunge would be anything but enjoyable.

A few minutes before two o'clock – the time fixed for starting – I strolled down to the bridge in question, and found a very large crowd assembled to view the proceedings. Shortly after, bands of men began to put in an appearance in the field against the bridge, which had hitherto been empty. They were prepared mostly as if for a deadly struggle; they wore thick nailed boots and leather gaiters, with padding underneath. When most of the players, over two hundred in number, had assembled in the centre of the field, they were harangued and told to do their duty. As the clock of the old church chimed two, the ball was thrown high up in the air, and the game commenced. The ball was not as other balls, which would have stood very few minutes under the severe treatment it received, but was made of cork on account of the water part of the proceedings, and covered with stout leather, which was painted red, white and blue in the brightest of hues, so that after the ball had been in the water a few times it was no slight thing either to kick it far in the first place, or to get a blow in the second. On the ball touching the ground again there was a great rush for it and hacks and blows were freely given and received. At first the ball made for the stream, and the onlookers' hopes rose high at the expectation of seeing the players floundering in the water, but they were doomed to be deferred for a short time, as by a well-directed rush the ball was forced through the gate into one of the principal streets of the town, along which it was carried for a short distance, and then down a narrow street into the playing fields, where it stayed for some time and a good deal of kicking and knocking about took place. The ball got nearer and nearer the stream, till at last in it and a number of players, went. This, of course, caused a good deal of amusement amongst the bystanders. The ball was rushed down the stream and a number of others joined the water party; as a matter of course many of them tumbled down. Now was the time to pay off old grudges, and it was apparently taken advantage of, for in several cases we saw men from one side roll players on the other unmercifully in the water, from which they arose soaked through and through. Another favourite practice appeared to be when a man was running down the stream with the ball – for they had been working down stream all this time – one of his opponents from the back would spring upon him and the chances were they would both get a good ducking; but this, in spite of the cold, never seemed to damp or cool their ardour. After splashing about in the stream for some time the ball was thrown on the bank again into the station yard, where there were some grand struggles among the trucks."

In the nineteenth century a great athletic revival took place and football clubs were formed by a number of the old public school boys. The year 1857 saw the Sheffield and Hallam Clubs started for the purpose of promoting the 'dribbling', or non-handling game; and in the following year the Blackheath and Richmond Clubs were instituted. Others followed in due course, and the dribbling game began to gain considerably in popularity, science and skill being preferred to the rough and often brutal methods of play which were formerly in vogue. An attempt was then made to determine upon a code of rules to govern all players. Although not at first successful, this led in a short time to the organisation of the Football Association, consisting of that numerous body which did not play according to the Rugby rules.

'Association' Football, of which these articles will principally treat, is easily described. The usual dimensions of the ground are 120 yards by 80, the goal posts being placed eight yards apart, with a crossbar, which is eight feet distant from the ground. In actual play only goals count and a goal is obtained (this explanation is only for our lady readers) when the ball is passed between the goal posts under the bar. The players are not allowed to handle the ball (with the exception of the goalkeeper) and may not carry it more than two steps. The sides number eleven each – goalkeeper, two backs, three half-backs and five forwards.

That the game still has its dangers cannot be denied and, in fact, the somewhat formidable list of casualties published each season has led many apprehensive people to decry football and to call for further modifications in the style of play. The late Wilkie Collins described the 'rage for muscular exercise' as a 'national eccentricity' and thought it responsible for much of the 'grossness and brutality among certain classes of the population'. The truth will probably be found lying between two extremes.

Overtraining and immoderate exertion are as mischievous in their effects as languor and sloth. In either case there must be a breakdown sooner or later. But healthful exercise and competitive sport need not ruin the body or blunt the mind. As for the accidents on the football field, which occasion the 'Lancet' so much concern, are not accidents equally painful, incident not only to every species of sport, but also to the performance of the commonest duties of life? They are so exceptional in character that little can be done to avoid them or to prevent their recurrence. And it is acknowledged that the more scientific the game the less danger can accrue; while considering the immense number of men continually at play the number of casualties cannot be cited as a proof that the sport is in itself of a specially riskful nature.

"Look at me", said Archie Hunter to me one day, when we were discussing this question, "look at me, and see if I am not a good example of the fact that football is not dangerous. Why, I have been playing now for eighteen years, ever since I was a boy at school and I have played all sorts of games with all sorts of players. Some of them in Scotland were colliers who could have knocked a bull down with a blow of their fists; and most of them had got arms like blacksmiths. Then in some of the most exciting matches, when every man is straining every nerve to win, you might expect that a bad kick or a severe tussle would lead to damage being done. Yet I never met with an accident in my life – except a slight injury to my right arm and I always reckon that I got that by my own fault. No, there is no danger in football if the real game is played. It is when the game is not played, and when the players are careless and unscientific, that they meet with accidents. I don't believe that the men who know how to play are ever hurt, unless they get stupid or are 'larking' on the field." With which observations I was profoundly impressed.

But these are not Archie Hunter's reminiscences, and it is time to get to them. This long digression was entered upon with the best intentions; but for all that it may be inexcusable. Anyhow, let us start a fresh paragraph and get to the subject. Or, better still, why not start a fresh chapter? Happy thought! It shall be done.

Chapter 2

Archie's First Exploits

"I was born," said Archie Hunter, as his faithful Squire and Penman sat himself down in a listening attitude by the famous skipper's side, anxious not to lose a word that was spoken – "I was born in the year 1859, at Joppa, which is not in Palestine, but is a quaint, old-fashioned little hamlet in Ayrshire, boasting only of one street, a kirk, and a few houses, with a score or so of people living in them. I was christened in gaol, which may not seem to have been a very good start in life."

"I hope you had not committed any very serious offence in your babyhood?" I remarked gravely.

"Oh, no," said Archie, laughing; "I was not a very desperate character at that time of life, being only a few weeks old. But I was christened in the courthouse of the prison because at that time the church was undergoing repairs and could not be used for the ceremony. Not far from Joppa my father had a farm, but he died while I was too young to remember him; and before I was many years older the family removed to Ayr, where I was sent to school. My three brothers – all dead now – were athletes, and I suppose the love of good, hearty games ran in our blood. The excellent country air, and the rural life we led, gave us plenty of strength and fitted us for out-door sports.

"It wasn't long before I was playing football at school with the other lads; but football in those days was very different to what it is now or ever will be again. There were no particular rules and we played pretty much as we liked; but we thought we were playing the Rugby game, of course, because the Association hadn't started then. It didn't matter as long as we got goals; and besides, we only played with one another, picking sides among ourselves and having friendly matches in the playground. Such as it was though, I got to like the game immensely, and I spent as much time as I could kicking the leather. We were a merry lot, but by and by I had to leave school while I was still very young, and I was rather sorry, I can assure you."

Here I nodded my head knowingly, as if to lead Archie to infer that I knew what a severe trial it was to leave school myself and could sympathise with him accordingly.

"Yes." said Archie, "I was sorry to go, but I wanted to continue playing, so I joined the Ayr 'Star' Football Club, which was then a Rugby Union team and for a short time I played the strict Rugby game. After playing the season under the Rugby rules we held a meeting, not, as you might think, in some comfortable room, but under the blue canopy of heaven, and by lamp-light; and after considerable discussion we determined to alter the name of the club from the 'Star' to the 'Thistle'. But there was soon to be a great change. The Queen's Park, the leading club in Scotland, adopted the Association rules almost as soon as they were made and of course, most of the other clubs began to follow the example. The 'Thistle' Club was one of them. I had only played in two matches under the old code, officiating as full back 'to the amazement and delight of my fellow-clubmates,' as one of the papers said; but now we began to practise dribbling."

"How did you like the change?" I asked.

"Very much," Archie responded, "So did all of us. And we went in for the new game with enthusiasm, I can tell you. Every other night saw us in hard training, and we learnt the art of working well together. In my opinion that is the secret of success. Good combination on the part of the players is greatly to be preferred to the muscular powers of one or two of them. Strength has got very little chance against science, and one of the most exciting matches we ever played proved that much once and for all."

"I should like to hear about it," I said.

"Well, it relates to the Mauchline Club, which was then the strongest club in Ayrshire, and one of the oldest clubs, too. Ours was but a young club and many of us who belonged to it were only youngsters also. The first time we met the Mauchline team they gave us a terrible beating – four goals to one. But we weren't going to be frightened, and the next season we met them again. There were some tremendous fellows on their side, colliers and others who looked like giants beside us. They looked down on us a bit, and thought they were going to have an easy win. But they didn't win at all. Not a bit of it. They found us a pretty tough lot and with all their strength – and a bit of roughness too – they could only score two goals to our three. I don't mind saying that every-body was a bit surprised at the form our side showed and at the result, but it was a very popular victory and we got no end of praise.

"The Mauchliners did not take their defeat with a very good grace however and when the winning goal was scored they protested against it and wanted it disallowed. When they found they couldn't have their own way they left the field in a body ten minutes before the finish and refused to return. But we met them again in following seasons, and they were friendly enough. Well, I consider that science triumphed over strength in that case and if you could have seen the difference between us and our opponents you would have thought so, too."

"And what did you do on this famous occasion?" was my next query.

"Oh, I played 'back' as before and got on pretty well. I like playing 'back' you know, and when I joined the Villa I asked for that position at first."

"Well, what else did the 'Thistles' do?"

"They played several good matches against first-class teams that year. We met Dunbreek, Lancefield, Kilburnie, Beith and Partick and de-feated them all. We had a hard struggle with Partick, drawing with them once and defeating them in a very close contest on the second try. In fact, it was wonderful to notice the rapid advance of the 'Thistle' Club. In a couple of seasons we came right into the front rank and this was accomplished only by sheer hard work and pluck. Cunningham was our captain and then Fullerton, who is now in South Africa. They made me captain the third season, although I could only have been between fifteen and sixteen years old."

"That was very young for such a position."

"Yes it was. I suppose I was one of the youngest captains of a first-class club ever known. But I want to tell you about the most remarkable match of all.

"In the year I speak of, Queen's Park had been defeated for the first time in the Scottish Cup Tie, losing to the Vale of Leven. They had won the Cup seven years in succession and the defeat was a heavy blow to them. It was rumoured that in this game the Vale of Leven team had worn spikes in their boots and as this came to the ears of the Association a committee was appointed to inquire into the truth of the allegation. The committee examined the ground and they found certain marks which tended to confirm the statement, but the evidence was not quite conclusive, and the Vale of Leven got the benefit of the doubt. Well, the defeat of Queen's Park left three clubs in the field for the semi-final, the Thistle, the Glasgow Rangers and the Vale of Leven. The Thistle was drawn against the Vale of Leven and the Rangers got the bye. The Ayr team were obliged to travel to Glasgow to play off the match and they did not arrive in very fresh and fit condition.

"As for me," Archie continued, "I didn't want to go. I was suffering from a sore foot and could not pull a boot on; but I was pressed very hard to accompany the team and at last I consented. When we got to the end of the journey, fatigued and not in the best spirits, we found that the snow was three or four inches thick on the ground and that altogether the conditions were most unfavourable for the game. But we'd got to play whether we liked it or not and play we did. The Vale at that time had the reputation of being the roughest players in Scotland; but in addition to that they were really a powerful team, well-accustomed to working together and thoroughly understanding the game. My foot was still so bad that I could only bear to have an old shoe on it. Fancy the state I was in on that sloshy field with one foot giving me pain and not even protected from the wet and cold! I was playing 'back' and though I don't think I missed a kick, I must say, that I didn't like the idea of kicking at all. It was fearful. But this was not the worst of our mishaps. Our goalkeeper had turned mutinous and we all believed that he was ready to sell the match.

"We had no other man to play in his place and whether our suspicion was true or not I can't say, but this I know: time after time he let the ball get past him without making the slightest effort to stop it. There were several very easy shots and there he stood with his hands down and allowed them to score. It made us all quite wild to see him. When we returned home after that eventful day's work I thought the people in the street would have done that goalkeeper harm. They had got to know all about him and were waiting for his return. I don't know how he escaped, but it was well for him that he did."

"And how did the game go?"

"Very evenly at first. We played up as well as we could and really we gave the Vale as much to do as they gave us. But there is no doubt, in my mind, that they were the better team and the only wonder is that we did as well as we did. I think that even if we had been playing our full strength they would have beaten us; as it was we came out of the contest creditably (with the exception named), but decisively beaten. And that ended our sport for that season."

"Did the Vale score again?"

"Oh, yes. They met the Glasgow Rangers and after two draws the Rangers withdrew, disputing the result and claiming to have won in the second encounter. So the Vale won the cup, but it was not a very popular victory. The 'Thistles' met the Rangers twice during the season 1877-78 and on each occasion the Glasgow team won, though they had to fight hard. All this time I was playing 'back,' except once, when I was put in as a 'left-wing man' in the place of an absentee."

"How did you get on?"

"Very well. I managed to score three goals out of five and I am glad to say that on that occasion we won the match."

"What was your style of play, Mr. Hunter?"

By way of reply Archie quietly put into my hand a paper, where I read these words: "His defence was of a different character to that adopted by the 'backs' generally. He always carefully noted his opponents' play and if a 'forward' eluded him once, the trick by which he did so was jotted down in his memory and seldom indeed was the performance repeated. Not often was it necessary for him to make a headlong rush and knock a forward deliberately off the ball. Weariness and watchfulness were the peculiar characteristics which brought him safely through many an awkward predicament, combined with a steady command of himself and a wonderfully quick eye to detect a weak point in the attacking division. Not only that, but hard and untiring practice was indulged in, drop-kicking and the knack of getting at the ball in almost any position were the especial features of his play and during the summer evenings, or on off-days, the team – amongst whom the favourite 'back' was always to be seen – went in for keeping themselves strictly in form and no opportunity was lost in bringing themselves into the best possible condition to meet the brother footballists on the field of fray."

"Is that report correct?" I asked.

"I suppose it is," replied Archie, with a smile. "I have nothing to add to it."

Archie was always modest.

Chapter 3

Scotchmen at Play

"I think," said Archie, speaking with great decision and looking as if he could defy the world to contradict him, "that there is no one to beat an Ayrshire man at football."

"That is a very bold statement," I ventured to remark, naturally with great humility.

"It is a bold statement," assented Archie, with a reassuring smile; "and don't think I have made it just because I'm an Ayrshire man myself. Nothing of the sort. I am simply thinking of the men I have met and who have distinguished themselves and I can't help being surprised at the number who have come from my own country. I can't explain it. I only know that the air is very bracing, that the country is open and that it is a healthy agricultural district producing some of the best cattle in the United Kingdom; and I suppose the people living there benefit by all these things. Why, I could give you plenty of names of famous players, if you wanted them."

"The very thing," I said. "Let us know something about the best men you have met."

"Very well. Have you ever heard of Bob Harrison?"

Here I blinked my eyes and said I should rather think I had.

"Bob was the most popular right wing I knew twelve or thirteen years ago. He played for the Kilmarnock Portland Club. A very good fellow was Bob. Then there was Higgins, also of Kilmarnock, a capital centre forward. Sam Thompson, centre forward in the Wolverhampton Wanderers, was an Ayrshire man. If you have never seen him play you had better go next time you have the chance. Then there was Watt, of Kilburnie; he played down at Perry Barr last year in the match for my benefit and he made a great impression as a right wing forward. I heard him spoken of very highly indeed; and don't forget to mention the two Goodalls, Archie and Johnnie, now playing with Derby. They are Kilmarnock men and everybody knows, I suppose, that Archie Goodall was playing for the Villa the year before last. He was very sorry to leave the Villa, but business drew him away and of course, he was obliged to go. There are two more Kilmarnock men worthy of mention also – Jemmy and Hugh Goodall, who belonged to the Kilmarnock Athletic Club. They were capital fellows and both good sportsmen – Jemmy in particular, who was a model goalkeeper. I shall never forget him as he used to stand between the posts, cool, collected and good-tempered, a giant of six feet two and never likely to miss a chance of keeping the ball from going through. He went home again about eight years ago, after playing for Darwen. Hugh was a very hard-working fellow on the field and played half-back or centre-forward. Poor chap! He's dead now. He caught a cold when he was out with his team and it never gave him a chance. He died very suddenly, to the regret of all who had met him."

"You have certainly made out a very good case for Ayrshire," I said.

"Oh, I could tell you of plenty more good players," said Archie, "only many of them are forgotten now and many more of them, though well known in Scotland, perhaps, were never able to make a reputation over here. But what makes all this so remarkable is that there is no profes- sionalism in Ayrshire – not a bit."

This was my grand chance. I don't know much about football, as I have frankly confessed, but I thought I could come out pretty strong just at this point.

"Of course not," I said, with airy confidence, "there is no profession- alism in Scotland." I noticed a peculiar look come into Archie's eyes – a very peculiar look, which was quite unaccountable. He seemed to be lost in deepest thought, and in this pensive state he continued for some time. Then I concluded I had better arouse him. So in the same light- hearted way I again remarked – "There is no professionalism in Scotland, Mr. Hunter."

"So I have heard," said Archie and again the peculiar look came into his eyes. I began to get suspicious. Was it possible that I could be mistaken? I don't know where I got the information from, but I have always believed that in bonny Scotland the football professional has no more existence than snakes have in Ireland. Was the faith of my youth about to be shattered, and the dream of a life-time ended: Verily it was. Archie came a bit closer and whispered – "There are dozens of professionals in Scotland. They may not be engaged openly and they may not be paid openly, but they are there all the same."

I felt grieved.

"Yes," continued Archie, "professional footballists are plentiful enough in Scotland and it is not much of a secret. Most people know what is going on. I see that an inquiry is just going to be made into the subject and no doubt all the truth will come out then."

"Well, do you think the practice will be stopped?" I asked, when I had recovered from the emotion which these painful confessions caused me.

"I don't think so for one moment," Archie replied. "On the contrary, I fully believe that before long the professional element in Scotland will be recognised and allowed. And a good thing for Scotland too! Why, the country is being drained continually of its best players and always will be as long as the present system exists. Directly a Scotchman proves himself a good player the agents have their eye on him and he gets an invitation to go over to England in a very short time. How can the game thrive in Scotland when this is done? Why, if it weren't for the enthusiasm that football provokes all over the country it would have been dead before now. That's my opinion."

"How do you account for so many Scotchmen being imported?"

"Well, there may be many reasons. First of all, you know, all Scotchmen are athletes. They develop plenty of muscle and they seem to get strength and stability from their mode of living and very often from the occupations also. Then they have a genuine love of the sport – a deep love for it which lasts a long time, not a passing fancy. They are different to many Englishmen in this way, who like cricket for a few seasons and then football for a few seasons and then something else for a few seasons. Scotchmen grow up playing football and they stick to it all their lives. They prefer it to all other outdoor sports. In some towns you may see all the boys playing football, although they have no shoes to their feet. I think the national character has something to do with their success. They are steady and persevering, and they always play to win. My experience of English players leads me to think that they can't be depended upon to do their best after a certain time. They will play excellently one season, or two, or three; but sooner or later their enthusiasm dies off and they get lazy, or want a change.

"Of course, I am speaking in very general terms now. I could tell you of dozens of Englishmen who are as good as the Scotch; but put the two bodies of players against one another and I think you will find the Scotch will come out better than the English.

"For all that, of course, there is a little jealousy displayed now and again over here against the northerners; and while the wholesale importation of Scotchmen is going on this is only to be expected. When the native prejudice against payment for sport has died out, there will be fewer of us over here playing in English matches and I repeat that I am sure that eventually professionalism will prevail in Scotland just the same as it does in England."

I commend these observations to all whom they concern and my commendation is quite disinterested, as I never expect to be engaged as a professional myself – or as anything else.

"You know," Archie continued with a smile, "they say we Scotchmen are everywhere. You've heard of the Englishman, I suppose, who was abusing the Scotch while being conducted through a Turkish camp by an officer named Hassan Bey, when the officer turned upon him and said, 'I'll tell ye what, ma mon, gin ye daur lowse yer tongue upon ma country like that. I'll gie ye a cloot o' the lug that'll mak' it tingle frae this to halloween.'

"'Good gracious,' said the Englishman, 'I thought you were a Turk.'

"'An' sae I am a Turk the noo, ma braw chiel',' retorted the irate Glasgow Mussulman, 'an' a better ane than ye'll ever mak' forbye; but when I gang hame (as I'll do or lang, if it be heaven's wull) I'll just be Wully Forbes, son o' auld Dady Forbes o' th' Gorbals, for a' that's come an' gane.' At that moment, a splendidly dressed Hungarian among the Russian officers, called out from the other bank of the stream, 'Wully, mon, there's a truce the noo, for twa hoors; just come we' me and we'll hae a glass o' whusky thegither'."

"Did you meet many good men in your early days, Mr. Hunter?" was my next question.

"Plenty," was the answer. "I can't remember them all just at this moment, but there were Tom Highet and Harry McNeil, the two finest left-wing forwards in Scotland in their day. They played for Queen's Park and helped to make that club the immense success it was. There never was anything to beat them in their particular play. They were irresistible. I doubt whether they ever had their equals as two wing men. Ah! I shan't forget them, I can assure you. I remember playing against them once. A picked team of Ayrshire met Queen's Park at Kilmarnock. Highet and McNeil played left-wing and I was full back. I had a hard time of it that day. You couldn't take the ball from them, struggle as you would. It was a stiff time for all of us, and we were beaten in the end, though we made Queen's Park fight hard for their victory, too.

"Another good player distinguished himself that day – James B. Weir, the Queen's Park right wing forward. I knew him very well. They called him the Prince of Dribblers, a name he fully deserved. I think he was the best forward in Scotland, and when he once got possession of the ball no one could take it from him. If you could have seen him play you would have remembered it. He was about twenty-three or twenty-four when I knew him and he played for Queen's Park seven or eight years. He was a merry fellow, always ready for fun and when the game was over no one liked a frolic better than he did. He wasn't afraid of a bit of hard work, either and he was brave as a lion, I remember one night in Glasgow a few of us were going home together and Jimmy Weir was in a fine, rollicking mood. He had been – well, celebrating a victory that day – and he was amusing us with his little pranks and his lively chatter.

We were all in the best of spirits and made a merry little party. All at once we were startled by a loud alarm in the street, and a cry of "Fire! Fire!". The people, excited as they always are on such occasions, began to run in the direction indicated by a red glare in the distance and we followed them. Sure enough a house was on fire and the flames were getting a firm hold on the building. Worse than that there were people in the house and already there was such a blaze that they found it hard to make their way to the doors.

"Presently, amid all the smoke and flame we saw a face at one of the topmost windows – a face that looked ghastly in the glare and was full of horror and despair. There were no ladders at hand and the lower part of the building was ablaze. It looked as if the poor creature – whether man or woman we could not distinguish – must be burnt to death in that furnace. Well, Jimmy was a carpenter by trade and I suppose he knew something about climbing up and down houses. What did he do but coolly commence to climb up a high wall, from which he could throw a rope to the poor creature who was in such terrible danger. We watched him go up and before very long – though it seemed a long time then – he managed to bring the poor thing down; and how he was cheered by the people to be sure! His heroism wasn't soon forgotten."

"It deserved to be remembered," I said.

"Among other good players I encountered," Archie continued, "were W. McKinnon, a very fine centre forward, Johnnie Key, a fine left-wing forward, noted for screwing a ball into goal, and Charlie Campbell, an exceedingly good half-back. Campbell played for seventeen or eighteen years and was the life and soul of the Queen's Park. That club would never have been the club it was if it had not been for his exertions; and its long period of unbroken success was largely owing to his powers of organisation and his own good play. He was captain of the club for many years and played many a fine game for his side, his special talent being displayed in the way he 'headed' the ball. Charlie was a right down good sort altogether, and was always ready to do any good turn he could for another player or another club. He had a very fair bass voice for singing and with some other members of the Queen's Park Club he founded an Amateur Dramatic Society; and they went about the neighbouring towns giving performances for the benefit of any club or member in distress. Rather good of them, wasn't it? They were able to render some very valuable assistance in this way to those who had fallen upon bad times or had had no luck or wanted a little bolstering up for some reason or other. Besides, they enjoyed themselves at the same time to a certain extent. Charlie was a very fluent speaker and had a tolerable share of humour; and he was very fond of music.

"He is still alive, I am glad to say, and is able to take a prominent part in the proceedings of the Association Committee while he still serves the old club of which he is such a devoted member by holding some honorary office in connection with it. I think they have made him President."

"He was an exceptionally long time playing, wasn't he?" I asked.

"Yes. Seventeen or eighteen years is very exceptional indeed. We don't often find a player last so long as that. Five years is the usual term. You see, when you play football hard and fast you are likely, in course of time, to sprain the joints of the knee or the thigh; and then you are no good afterwards. I have known men who have suffered in this way, and who have thought they were cured and able to play again. But the first time they have tried to kick hard they have collapsed. If the joints once go, a man ought never to try and play any more.

"Well, if you want to make a list of the best players in Scotland – I am speaking of the period between 1876 and 1878 – I don't think you should omit to mention my brother John, though of course, you might not think it becoming for me to talk about him much. But he was a very strong 'back', he played for about ten years with the 3rd Lanark Volunteers. He distinguished himself in several International matches, and more notably still in two matches against the Dumbarton Club, the first of which ended in a draw and the second in a decisive victory for the Lanark by three goals to one. My brother also took his part in seve-ral 'four-a-side contests,' which were competitions for medals. In these contests you may explain for those who may not know, there was no goalkeeper and the four players on either side were two forwards, a half-back and a back. 'Four-a-side contests' were very useful for showing the skill and speed and judgement of the players and John Hunter made many a good display in them. There are two other Scotchmen I ought not to forget: Gillespie, who played 'back' for the Glasgow Rangers, and who now plays goalkeeper for Queen's Park; and Joe Taylor, who played a very fast game as 'full-back' for Queen's Park in those days – both excellent men."

"Does this complete the list?"

"By no means. I've got to tell you of a very important player now, Fergus Suter, 'Fergie' as we call him, came to England in the same year as myself; and we two led the 'Scotch Exodus,' as it has been called. Fergie was a Glasgow man and he commenced his football career by playing the Rugby game when he was very young. When he went over to the Association side he started as a 'forward,' but ever since I have known him he has played 'back' and a grand 'back' he is. He belonged to the Partick Club and then became a member of the Glasgow Rangers; and in 1878 he went to Darwen and practically taught that club the game. He travelled to London to fight for the Association Cup, but after three attempts his team was beaten.

"He was best known, however, as one of the strongest supports of the Blackburn Rovers and he played a very fine game. I met him many times and always found him honest and good-hearted on the field. He won a large number of gold and silver medals and it is said that he played for Lancashire against every English county. He took part in all the ties in which the Rovers were engaged, and helped his club to defeat Queen's Park and West Bromwich Albion and win the cup.

"Then there is Ross, an Edinburgh man, called 'the little demon,' on account of his quick, smart play. He was a grand shot at goal and is still playing for Preston North End. He played for a time, however, with the Everton, but the Preston Club was his first love. His brother – familiarly known as 'Nick' Ross – (it is nice, isn't it, to have a 'Nick' and a 'Demon' in the same family?) was practically the man who brought Preston North End into notoriety. He was a 'full back' and played splendidly. Last of all, though by no means least, there is Alexander Latta, of the Everton team, whom I well remember taking a notable part in the International contests, Scotland versus Wales and Scotland versus England. He is a Dumbarton man and the next remarkable thing to his play is that he doesn't drink or smoke.

"Now don't think," said Archie, hastily, "that I mean to suggest that the majority of football players are intemperate, or that they are given to over-indulgence either with ale or tobacco. There is an impression abroad – especially among those who don't know anything about the game and the players – that after every match the members go to the nearest tavern and drink as hard as they can. Well, you may find them in a tavern, because it is usual to reassemble in some convenient place; but I deny that footballers on such occasions go beyond proper limits. On the contrary, they are very moderate indeed in this way. The fact is they are obliged to be, or they would be no good. When in strict training they can't be too careful; and though a man who is accustomed to having a glass of ale at his dinner is not forbidden to take it, yet if he can do without it he is told to abstain. Any recklessness in drinking and smoking would soon tell upon a player, and you wouldn't see him playing very long. Though it is unusual to find a man both a teetotaller and a non-smoker, yet it is not uncommon to find a man either the one or the other; and I should like my experience in this respect to be known."

"It shall be known," I said as I faithfully jotted down the Villa Captain's words.

"And now," said Archie, "I have related all that there is worth knowing of my life in Scotland and have told you all whom I met there. The most important part of my career is that which followed. I was sorry to leave my home, but it was business that took me away. I had been apprenticed to the hardware trade and I wanted to get a better insight into the business, so I came to Birmingham. My old club, the 'Thistle' presented me with a testimonial when I was about to leave and gave me a ring and a gold Albert chain. There was a large gathering of my old comrades and friends and the captain of the club and others, made many complimentary speeches, which was very generous of them. (By the way, the 'Thistle' club exists no longer. Its greatest opponents were the Ayr 'Academicals' and soon after I left the two clubs amalgamated and called themselves by the name of the county; and they are now the strongest club in the district.) So I left Scotland and came to Birmingham, arriving on the 8th August, 1878. I hadn't a single friend in the town and I ..."

"Thank you, Mr. Hunter," said I, gathering up my papers, "we'll leave that until next week."

Chapter 4

The Rise of Aston Villa

"As I was saying when you interrupted me so sharply," said Archie Hunter, as he settled himself down for a chat. "I came to Birmingham on 8th August 1878. It was the first time I had crossed the border and I wasn't in the best of spirits. Remember, I was still under twenty.

"The journey down was a long and dull one and when I got out at the station I saw none but strange faces. I hadn't a single friend to meet me and I knew no one belonging to the firm by whom I had been engaged. It was Saturday and of course, the town was busy and bustling and every man had got enough to do without taking any notice of a lonely Scot. I walked out of the railway station, not knowing where to go, or where any of the streets led to. But I wandered on, past the Parish Church and through Digbeth, until at last I came to a park, Adderley Park, I afterwards found was its name. There was a cricket match being played there, so I walked in and watched it all the afternoon; and so my first day in Birmingham passed away.

"Of course, things brightened up afterwards and I soon made many friends and got to like the town. But I must say that my first impression of Birmingham was not a very good one.

"While I was in Scotland I had become acquainted with the Calthorpe Football Club, which used to come up and play the second team of Queen's Park. There were some very fair players in the Calthorpe and I made up my mind, on arriving in Birmingham, to join them. But one of my fellow-workmen, George Uzzell, mentioned Aston Villa to me as a club that had come rapidly to the fore and asked me to become a member of it. I hesitated for some time, but at last my friend told me that a 'brither Scot,' Mr. George Ramsay, was the Villa captain and that decided me. Mr. Ramsay was a Glasgow man and had exerted himself very considerably to bring the Villa team into the front rank. He was himself a good right-wing forward and was well supported by W. B. Mason. So to Mr. Ramsay I went and we at once became good friends and remain so to this day.

"Mr. Ramsay was practically the founder of the Aston Villa Football Club. He had had good tuition in the game while in Scotland and as a member of the 'Oxford' Club he had gained plenty of experience and taken part in several first-class matches. A short time before he left, his club had tied three times with the Glasgow Rangers for the Scotch Cup. He was keeping goal and he relates that on the last occasion he saved his goal at the expense of a broken nose.

"Mr. Ramsay was a capital all-round player and could take any position and give a good account of himself. Coming to Birmingham he found football here in a very backward state. The four principal clubs were St. Mary's, Aston Unity, Calthorpe and the Birmingham. One day Mr. Ramsay saw a few lads playing together in the big public park facing Park Road, Aston and he watched them with some amount of curiosity and amusement. They were connected with the Villa Cross Wesleyan Chapel and only had the most primitive ideas of the game. Mr. Ramsay describes their play as 'a dash at the man and a big kick at the ball;' they were entirely ignorant of dribbling and were evidently in the most rudimentary stage of knowledge – quite 'juvenile,' as Mr. Ramsay said.

"Well, when he had watched the lads some time he spoke to a bystander and suggested that they two should join in the game. Then he called to one of the players, William Weiss by name and proposed that he should be allowed to play on one side and his chance acquaintance on the other. When his broad Scotch had, after much trouble, been understood, the proposal was agreed to and Mr. Ramsay began to play. He soon showed that science was superior to all their big kicks and easily dribbled the ball past the men who had never seen a display of the kind before. They were amazed when they saw how he played and when all was over they surrounded the player, who had footed the ball so neatly and asked him a hundred questions. So pleased were they with the newcomer's performance that they besought him to play for them in their next match which was arranged for the following week. This was against Stafford Road, which had beaten the young Villans in a previous contest by 7 goals to 0; and the latter were anxious to have their revenge. Mr. Ramsay set himself the task of teaching his comrades how to play the scientific game, a labour of some difficulty; but he was so far successful that when the match came off the Stafford Road had to struggle hard for the victory and only scored a single goal."

"Mr. Ramsay, or 'Scotty' as he was called, had so far distinguished himself that he began to receive invitations from all the clubs in the district to play for them. But he had taken a strong liking for his first friends and had an idea that he could make something of them.

"They elected him their captain and he set to work to teach them dribbling. His material consisted of such men as W. B. Mason (now Birmingham representative to the National Association), Such, Lees, Hughes, Smith, Price, Weiss, Scattergood, Midgley and others – very few of whom still don the jersey. Later on they were joined by the Lindsays (two Scotchmen), Stevens, Law, O'Connor, Johnstone, Apperley and Pank, who with perseverance and careful study of the more scientific game had formed themselves into a very decent little team and begun to make a name for themselves.

"They began to want a field of their own to play in; a meeting was held and it was decided to look out for suitable ground. Although it was by no means in a perfect condition, the ground at Perry Barr was taken and Mr. Ramsay gives an amusing account of how, after an hour's hot debating, he offered £5 for the use of the field for that season; how £10 was demanded and another long discussion took place and was ultimately ended by the two sides agreeing to split the difference.

"The first gate resulted in the sum of 5s. 3d. (five shillings and three pence), being added to the funds of the club. But still the club went on and made a name for itself. Sometimes a gate of nearly £10 was obtained, but this was exceptional. In the meantime expenses were increasing. The ground was taken on a three years' lease, rising from £7 10s. to £15 and then to £20. This lease had scarcely run out when the ground was to be taken for building purposes. A meeting of the club was called and a statement of affairs drawn up, when it was found the finances were rapidly increasing. It was resolved to make a dreadful plunge and go straight to headquarters, which was done, with the result that the ground was taken on a seven years' lease at £100 per annum. In the meantime," continued Archie, "I had come down and had joined the club under the circumstances I told you."

"The first match in which I played for the Villa – and the first I ever played in England – was rather remarkable. It was called a 'friendly' match, but that term must only be considered in the professional sense. It was the most unfriendly affair in which I ever took part. Our opponents were the Burton Robin Hoods, and we Villa men journeyed to Burton to meet them. It was quite evident to us from the beginning that nobody in Burton wanted us to win that match and that they were determined to do their best to prevent our succeeding. We didn't have a very good reception and whenever we played up well there was a howl of disapprobation from the spectators. We went on all the same and were not going to be intimidated; and as a matter of fact, we soon showed that we were superior to our rivals.

"When we scored our first goal the blood of the Robin Hoods began to get up. They played a rough game, but we put it down to excitement and went on. I can't say it was altogether enjoyable, because it is one thing to have a hard fight and another thing to fight like savages. Well, presently we scored a second goal and that stirred up the rage of the Robin Hoods more than ever and the wrath of the spectators was as a consuming fire.

"What do you think the people did? They got between the goal posts, some hundreds of them, forming a solid background and presently, when a shot was made, the ball rebounded back into play and the Robin Hood claimed that no goal had been scored. That was all very well for them, but we disagreed. It was 'Evergreen' Sammy Law, the centre forward, who had made the winning kick and we rallied round him. But the umpire would not allow the goal, so, as a protest, we left the field.

"I was not sorry to get away, for during the course of the game one of the Burton players had so far lost control of himself that he made sudden dashes in my direction and chased me all over the field. He had his sleeves turned up and every time he came near me he doubled up his fists in a very ominous manner. I thought he meant business, but fortunately, I was able to avoid him and escaped with my life."

"What had you done to incur his anger?"

"Well, I suppose I hadn't let him take the ball from me, you see and had been making rings round him. He was evidently a disappointed man and wanted to show me the evil consequences of playing as well as I could for my own side, but I wasn't disposed to take a lesson. Yes, it was a very queer match altogether, especially for a 'friendly' one. But it was the only one of the sort I played. Being my first match in England, of course, it gave me a rather bad impression of how things went on over here, but subsequent events caused me to alter my opinion.

"The Villa now entered upon a very important era. Our season was a brilliant one and we were only beaten twice – first by the second team of the Queen's Park, which was then captained by David Anderson, by three goals to two, which match had been arranged through the personal influence of Mr. Ramsay, who knew the Glasgow men well and who was then upon a holiday. He tried to get their first team down, but Captain Charles Campbell told him they had better take the second team first and if we could beat them he would arrange for the first team to visit us the following year.

"Our second defeat was by the Aston Unity, in the first round of the Birmingham Cup, by one goal to nothing. We considered the Aston Unity our big opponents at that time. The team was captained by Butler, who played a splendid game as full back; but unhappily he was overtaken by a terrible infliction resulting in the total loss of his eyesight and it is said he will never recover from his blindness. Before him Hundy was captain and the club remained very strong and as I have said they beat us in the first cup tie. I ought to tell you something more about the ground at Perry Barr which we played on in those times. It was covered pretty thickly with trees and the players had to run 'round about and in and out' of them, in order to get at the ball. It was very amusing, but it didn't always conduce to scientific play. When we first played there were two trees on each side of the ground which served as goal-posts and there were trees on the touch line.

"As the Villa Club rose funds were obtained to clear the ground and once it was thought of making it into a running track. The trees were cut down and the roots blown up by dynamite and what was left of them after that soon disappeared. I suppose the timber came in useful as firewood for the people in the locality.

"We played about six matches in connection with the Cup tie, and won very easily. For example, in the match against the Small Heath Swifts we won by twenty-two goals to none; and some humourist fetched our goalkeeper, Copley, a chair to sit upon, as he had nothing at all to do and was getting tired of standing and never having a chance of a kick. But the Aston Unity were too strong for us.

"I may mention one incident in our match with them which shows how players are sometimes carried away by excitement. While I shot for goal the ball skimmed the bar and the Unity goalkeeper immediately caught me round the neck, held me fast and seemed about to deliver a tremendous blow at my face. Everybody saw it; but my rival recovered himself in time and afterwards offered the fullest explanation of his action. I am quite convinced that he had no deliberate intention of doing me any personal injury; he simply lost his self-control for a moment and was unable to restrain himself. In football there are many temptations of this sort and it requires a great amount of goodhearted-ness and coolness to refrain from taking advantage of the proximity of an opponent.

"But the best players set their faces very sternly against roughness of all kinds, and some of the finest footballers I know are the most gene-rous and good-natured of men on the field. I don't think much advantage is ever gained by bad temper or spiteful play. If one man is rough, another recriminates; and if one side shows bad blood, the other side is sure to have its bad blood stirred up also. You can play to win and play with perfect fairness; that is my experience.

"In 1880 we won our first cup, viz: the Birmingham Challenge Cup, Mr. Ramsay kicking the only goal (after a terribly hard struggle) three minutes before the finish and wasn't there a scene? Hats, sticks and umbrellas were flying in all directions, almost darkening the air.

"The next season I was elected captain, Mr. Ramsay nominating me to fill his position. He resigned on account of business engagements which prevented him devoting the necessary time to football. He was then presented with a handsome gold Albert chain in appreciation of his past invaluable services. He had been playing football for thirteen years and during that time he had played in every position in the field. He was good at football races also and won a special prize in a quarter-mile race, in connection with the Birmingham Cup Sports. He played against Wales in 1878, when he captained the Birmingham team and in nearly all the Association matches between 1877 and 1879.

"His interest in the club has always been maintained and his record is remarkable. He may justly claim to have been the founder of the Aston Villa and to have taught the game to its first members. At one time he was chairman of the committee, the Villa representative on the Association, the leader in many deputations and for the last four years the club's secretary. We owe a great deal to Mr. Ramsay as a club and as individuals and his name is indissolubly connected with the history of the club.

"I was playing centre forward at this time and only on two occasions took up my old position as back – once against Stafford Road and once against Stoke. My play on each of these occasions gave great satisfaction. In the match against Stafford Road we won by one goal to nought and the match against Stoke resulted in a draw.

"One of the football writers said: 'It was only Archie Hunter's splendid defence and indomitable energy which saved the team from defeat.' We now began to be more talked about than ever and very great things were expected and prophesied of the Villa. The club had grown greatly in strength and had naturally become ambitious.

"My brother Andy, who had been playing with the Third Lanark Volunteers, came down from Scotland and Eli Davis, Teddy Lee, Tom Pank, Sammy Law, Howard Vaughton, Arthur Brown and W. Crossland were the other members of the team. We had a most exciting year and gained a remarkable record, winning nineteen matches and losing only one. We had every reason to be proud of our successes, for we finished by carrying off the Birmingham Cup, defeating Saltley College in the final; and we were within an ace of winning the Staffordshire Cup also, but were beaten right at the finish. All the team were playing well together at this time and working hard and the next season we determined, if possible, to beat even the splendid record we had just made."

Chapter 5

Play Up, Villa

"Perhaps if I tell you something of the team as it was then composed you will be interested," said Archie, "and it will give me an opportunity of paying a tribute which they well deserve to my old comrades."

"Your 'co-mates and brothers in exile,' I suppose," I remarked, thinking that the Villa captain would appreciate a little Shakespeare.

"Certainly," he said, when I had repeated the phrase several times at his request. "There are few of them playing now. Most of them are on the retired list, but although they do not play, you are sure to see them among the most interested of the spectators whenever an important match is played. Football is a life-devotion. I am constantly coming across old friends and seeing familiar faces whenever I stroll down to the ground. We fight the old battles over again in our talk, discuss tremendous kicks, recall a famous shot for goal and give and receive news of those who have wandered away. There are some very unexpected meetings, I can assure you and messages and greetings are always being carried along from field to field by mutual friends.

"Of course, in a few cases there are players who go away and are lost sight of altogether; and I am sorry to say that in our own team death has made havoc within the last few years. My brother is an example. He was a great favourite down here and took my place as captain of the Villa team when I was absent. Perhaps you won't mind if I tell you something of him first. In Scotland he played with the Lancelot Club, of which Hugh McIntyre was also a member. Mr. McIntyre was one of the first Scotchmen imported into this country and was captain of the Blackburn Rovers during the three years they held the English Cup. He afterwards joined the Glasgow Rangers and about the same time Andy became a member of the Third Lanark Volunteers, playing right wing for them.

His style was characterised by tremendous speed and it was splendid to see him centre the ball. Although he suffered greatly with his knee coming out of joint he always played a plucky game.

"Business took him back to Ayr for a time and then I was fortunate enough to get him down here to play for the Villa. His first match was against the Walsall Swifts and that day he played a grand game in his old position as right-wing and immediately he sprang into prominence. He played with us regularly, and with great success until he caught a severe cold on the field and we had to send him abroad. That was in August 1884. Much regret was manifested at his departure and I remember a local bard breaking out into verse and a few of the lines ran:

Why stay to laud him, the erstwhile right wing,
What need o'er his virtues to scan?
Those who best know him are loudest to sing
His praises as player and man.
Andy Hunter is going, we hope that his ship
May healthy and sound bring him back;
A smile and a tear and a muscular grip –
Bon voyage to the Perry Barr crack!

Our hopes, however, were not realised and Andy never returned.

"Another special favourite with the spectators was Eli Davis, who worked the left wing and was noted for the really wonderful way in which he screwed the ball from the corner with his left foot. As everybody knows, a forward is not much good unless he can take the ball up and centre it in goal, and in doing this Eli excelled. He was a very brilliant and a very sure player. In those days it was the rule to throw the ball with one hand only, not with two as is now the custom; and Eli, who was left-handed, had a very clever knack of throwing the ball from the touch-line right through goal. A great cheer always used to greet this performance.

"One of the best of our all-round men was Howard Vaughton, a very popular athlete. Skating, rinking, cycling and football were all in his programme and his good-tempered smile, no matter how hard his work, won for him a host of friends. He was a very busy sportsman – a regular 'flyer'. One night, for example, he was in London with some merry-making comrades and the next morning he was in Liverpool, just arriving in time to play in a Cup tie and before many minutes had elapsed he shot the leather through the goal. He surprised everyone one day by winning a three miles bicycle handicap, heading the leader in the last lap and rushing by him as if moved – as someone said – by an electric motive power.

"He was equally surprising on the football field. Sometimes he would let the easiest chance of scoring go by and at other times he would come out victorious from what seemed a thoroughly hopeless scrimmage. Lots of misses must be placed to his record, but he always atoned for them by thoroughly brilliant performances. Once, when we were play-ing Derby, he scored two goals in masterly style. On the second of these occasions I had lost sight of him altogether among a crowd of the Derby players and could only tell he was there by an occasional glimpse of his jersey. Then I saw him right under the bar with his toe at the ball and he dribbled past the goalkeeper amidst a perfect torrent of applause.

"Tom Pank, a capital half-back, was a sprint runner and being exceed-ingly fast did excellently in the position assigned to him. It was no unusual thing for him to overtake a player who had got past him and return the ball to field. He was very strong and very quick and his oppo-nents were never quite sure but that he would 'collar' them again although he had been left behind.

"Then there was Sammy Law, a smart player, who was our centre for-ward at first and afterwards did good service as half-back. Teddy Lee, one of the oldest members of the Villa, had not his equal as a half-back at that time. He was remarkably stubborn in his tackling of the ball and fought to the death. I should not call him a first-class scientific player, but he fed his forwards well and by pluck and perseverance and by refusing to allow himself to be beaten, he accomplished a great deal.

"Oliver Whately was a hard worker and a clever player. He was the life and soul of the Villa team, being a good singer, one who could play the piano as well and was always a merry, good-tempered comrade. He came from the Aston 'Florence' team and improved greatly during his stay with us, becoming ultimately one of the best forwards in the field and a deadly shot at goal. He was appropriately entitled the 'Daisy-cutter' as he always kept the ball low on the ground. He and Andy on the right were invincible.

"In those days we played six forwards, three half-backs, and only one back and that one back was Harry Simmonds, a good tackler with a very powerful kick. He was noted for his coolness and always met his opponents with judgement and courage.

"Another man with tremendous leg power was Arthur Brown, who came from the Aston Unity and played centre forward with me. He distinguished himself most, I think, when playing against his old club. The ground was very heavy that day, but the Unity team had no chance at all. We scored fifteen goals and Brown was credited with nine or ten of them.

"Then there was Crossland, Andy's partner and backer-up as a right wing forward. His best performance was against the Wednesbury Old Athletics, when he scored three goals out of six. Latterly, he sprained his knee and had to give up playing.

"I suppose you know that accidents of this sort are most common to us footballers. For instance, my brother Andy's knee used to come out of the socket in the course of nearly every match we played, but after I had pulled it in again he went on playing just as if nothing had happened. Of course, it got worse and worse as time went on and sometimes it took fully ten minutes before he was ready again. This happened when we were about to play the Walsall Swifts – his knee came out the first time he touched the ball during a little practice before the game began. That was a very unlucky match for us altogether. Our team was not very fit at the commencement, then the accident happened to Andy and later on Copley, the goalkeeper, was struck with the ball in the face and was seen for the rest of the afternoon with a bleeding nose. We lost the match and were thoroughly out of spirits.

"Copley came from Saltley College; he was nimble and strong and just the right man for keeping goal. Once, when we were playing Notts County, on Trent Bridge Ground, he saved his goal in a miraculous manner. He was on the ground and there were three or four on the top of him. We saw him struggle to his knees, then he was tumbled over, but he stuck to the ball and eventually got it into play again.

"There is one more player to mention – Billy Roberts, a Welshman, who joined us later on and played with Eli Davis. He was called 'Eli's labourer' on account of the hard work he did in feeding Eli, who would then centre the ball into goal. Roberts was a good fellow and immensely popular, for he was full of fun and caused many a roar of laughter by his amusing antics on the field.

"These, with George Ramsay, whom I specially mentioned last week, comprised our team for the season 1879-80; and I have told you all this about the individual players in order that you may have a fair idea of the sort of material we had to work with. We were full of ambitious plans and were determined not to be easily beaten. Three Cups were entered for: The English Cup, the Birmingham Cup and the Staffordshire Cup, but only the last was won. Stafford Road beat us for the English Cup by three goals to two and I attribute that defeat purely to bad luck. Andy had to stand out of the team that day owing to illness and one or two others were disabled. I myself was playing with my arm in a sling, having received an injury the previous week. The match was played at Perry Barr and our supporters had rallied round us fully expecting that we should win. The reverse we experienced was a thorough knock-back. Still, we had to take our luck as it came, you know; and fortunately we had full compensation afterwards.

"I'll tell you how we scored off the Wednesbury Old Athletics in the semi-final. They were a very strong team and had a good record and they came over to play us at the Lower Grounds, Aston. A strong, big set of fellows they were and had so little an idea of being defeated by us that they came over with ribbons flying and brought with them a band playing triumphal music. A great concourse of Black Country people followed them to see us defeated and to cheer their victorious comrades and there was great excitement on the ground, it being reckoned that altogether 14,000 people were present. It was an immense crowd and we felt that we were being put upon our mettle. the Wednesbury 'Old Uns' received a vociferous cheer when they entered the field, but encouraging shouts of 'Play up, Villa' came from our own supporters. And we did play up and soon one goal, then two, then three were placed to our account. Our own supporters cheered us loudly and I may mention that one enthusiast, who had climbed up a lamp-post to view the game, was so carried away with excitement that he loosed his hold on purpose to applaud and immediately fell to the ground with a crash; but he was not hurt and the incident provoked the greatest hilarity.

"The 'Old Uns' began to look green and put forth all their strength, even becoming rather rough at times, but still we played on and presently a magnificent shot put another point in our favour. We changed sides and went on, the struggle becoming fiercer and fiercer and our opponents evidently realised that they would have to score sure and fast if they were to avert disaster.

"Just then there was a tremendous crash and a roar of confused voices. All the players stopped dead to see what was the matter. Well, hundreds of people who had been standing on the roof of the dressing room had suddenly disappeared! The roof had given way under their weight. There was intense excitement and for a time the game was at a standstill until we knew whether a serious disaster had happened or not. Fortunately, no one was much injured and then we renewed our play.

"Would you believe it, the 'Old Uns' never scored at all that day. No! The men who had come with flags and ribbons and a brass band and a huge concourse of friends, went home again in mourning – beaten by six goals to none. They put up the shutters next day – well, it was Sunday and that might have been the reason. But the Villa reckon that among their famous victories.

"We lost the Birmingham Cup to the Walsall Swifts under rather curious circumstances. We had met many strong teams and proved ourselves their equal or better – Blackburn Rovers, Darwen, Notts Forest, Wednesbury Strollers and others – and we thought there was no particular need to be afraid of the Swifts. But it happened that in coming over in a brake to play us in the final cup tie at the Lower Grounds they were upset and some of the members shaken. Being told this we determined to spare them and the order was given not to press them too severely. Well, twenty minutes after the start the Swifts scored; then they got instructions to line their goal and a regular bombardment took place, which lasted to the finish. We had to be more severe at the end and we stretched out two of our opponents, but could not score, though we often came very near to doing so. A miss, however, is as good – or as bad – as a mile and there we were, defeated by one goal to nothing. In the opinion of some people the match was not played with the fairness which could give complete satisfaction. Some bad temper was displayed on the field, and the Villa men were greatly nettled at being defeated. But the very next week brought its revenge.

"We were drawn to meet the Swifts the following Saturday in the final tie of the Staffordshire Cup and I need scarcely tell you that we went over to Stoke, where the match was to be played, with a full determination of winning if we possibly could. Well, we fairly smothered them, scoring four goals to a single and on that day I was able to perform a little with the ball myself. I dribbled it past man after man and took it right into goal, three out of the four points being placed to my credit. All our men played with a dash and skill which simply broke down the defence of the Swifts and we showed what determination could do. It was a memorable day for us and our victory was a most popular one.

"On New Year's Day 1881, the Villa met the Heart of Midlothian team at Perry Barr and scored a decisive and brilliant victory. Winning the toss, we gained the double advantage of playing downhill and of having the wind in our favour. The game was, however, very stubbornly contested and after we had scored one goal fortune favoured us again and a miskick by one of the Northerners enabled me to get the ball between the posts a second time. The Scotchmen tried their best to take advantage of the kick-off and an excellent run was only stopped by Pank, whose superior speed once more served us well. A passing run, in which I took part, helped us immediately afterwards to score a third goal. Up and down field the ball was rapidly carried and for some time the chief play was confined to the forwards of either team, our fortress being often endangered and a foul close to the Villa goal gave the Scotchmen a good opportunity of doing well. But Pank cleared away the ball and the Villa went with a rush for the ball and after a scrimmage our fourth goal was obtained. On resuming after half-time the Hearts played a more accurate game, but the back division of the Villa was so much faster than the Edinburgh forwards that scoring was no easy matter. There were several good runs in the course of the game and at last the Scotchmen spurred themselves for the last effort and Lees and Alexander (forwards) deftly passed the backs and cleverly scored. When time was called, however, the Villa had won by 4 goals to 2.

"A more important match was played the following Saturday with Darwen, the Manchester team journeying down to Perry Barr to meet us. This match excited more than ordinary interest among lovers of the dribbling game from the fact that each club was then the holder of the Challenge Cup of the respective district association to which it belonged.

"The previous week, too, the Northern team had met our old antagonists, the Wednesbury Old Athletic and beaten them. At the time fixed for the commencement of the game with us the field was lined all round with a dense crowd of spectators and over five thousand people had paid for admission to the grounds. Outside, every point from which a glimpse of the game could be obtained was crowded with eager sightseers.

"The strangers won the toss and elected to play the first half up-hill. On the ball being kicked off it was secured by the Darwen left wing forwards and quickly carried with wide swift passing up the field and sent in front of our goal. We did not let it stay long there, you may be sure and after a bit of even play the Villa forwards made the first attempt to score from a centre by my brother Andy; but the Darwen goalkeeper (Broughton) averted the shot by sending the ball over the line. The corner kick, taken by Andy, was well-judged, but again the ball was got away; but Andy, with a good shy, landed the leather right into the mouth of goal and in the scrimmage a rush by Vaughton and Eli Davis carried it through the posts, thus securing the first goal within ten minutes from the commencement of the game. This put us in excellent spirits and Andy, who was playing a grand game, took the ball right down the Darwen lines in fine form, but the corner kick was unsuccessful. Then the Darwen got a chance and for some time kept the ball in close and dangerous proximity to our goal, but Vaughton and Davis managed to work it slowly into the opposition territory. Getting into the corner, Davis finished with a fine left foot centre and as the ball came across the point of the Darwen charge, Brown cleverly met it with his head, sending it flying into the goal. In vain the goalkeeper tried to stave off the unexpected attack. Before he could get at the ball it struck the underside of the crossbar sharply and rebounded to the ground and through the posts. This was our second point and caused much enthusiasm.

"On resuming play the Manchester forwards showed great dash and several times looked dangerous, but the swiftness of the Villa half-backs, combined with the sure kicking and tackling of Simmonds, neutralised all their efforts. Once, Eli Davis sent in a swift oblique shot which caused the spectators to raise shouts of 'goal', but the ball was just a trifle high, and went skimming along the crossbar of the Darwen goal, much too near to be pleasant to the custodian. Soon after Davis shied the ball right across the mouth of the goal and just as everyone expected to see it go over the line, Andy met it with a finely judged screw kick and scored splendidly, the people loudly cheering this feat. Simmonds, playing back, distinguished himself next. The kick from the centre gave Rostron, one of the Darwen forwards, the ball and he put on a fine dodging run in the centre, taking his charge clean past the Villa half-backs. Simmonds was the only man, excepting the goalkeeper, whom he had to meet and with a clear field before him he dribbled the ball straight for goal. At first, when Simmonds tried to stop him, he dodged and got away, but the Villa back was not yet defeated and returning quickly, he cleverly tackled Rostron just as the latter was judging his shot and passed the ball to Davis and Vaughton, who took it into the Darwen ground.

"Ends were changed and we scored a fourth goal after an exciting run and this took some of the dash out of Darwen, who now seemed to regard their chance of winning as hopeless. Andy continued to play remarkably well and shot several times for goal and the Darwen goal-keeper was kept very busy indeed for some time. He displayed great skill, agility and quickness of eye and his play at this point called forth the cheers of the spectators time after time. Towards the end of the game we began to get rather careless and several good chances were missed; but just as Vaughton had got the ball at his feet with an obviously clear course for goal, time was called and we were victorious by four goals to nil.

"The Darwen team, I ought not to omit to tell you, were captained by Mr. Hindle, who played a magnificent game throughout. Those who saw this match may be interested in recalling the names of those who took part in it:- Aston Villa: Copley, (goal); Simmonds (back); Law, Lees and Pank (half-backs); Eli Davis, Howard Vaughton, Archie Hunter (captain); Brown, Crossland and Andy Hunter (forwards). Darwen: Broughton (goal); Hindle (captain) and Murray (backs); Morehouse and Duxbury (half-backs); Marshall, Rostron, Kirkham, Marsden, Bury and Mellor (forwards)."

Chapter 6

"Foot it Featly Here and There" – Shakespeare

"Ah, yes," said Archie, in answer to a question of mine, "I met some capital fellows during these seasons in the course of our contests. Although there was occasionally a little ill-feeling on the field and perhaps a little roughness in the excitement of the moment, when the game was over we were soon all friends again. Take them for all in all footballers are a sociable and good-tempered lot.

"I well remember Moon, captain of the Wednesbury Old Athletics, against whom I often played. He was a most persevering centre forward and now that his days of harder work are over he is acting as referee and is well qualified for the position. His successor as captain was George Holder, who played right wing forward and a splendid exponent of the game. He was speedy and scientific and gained international honours. The names of these two will be very familiar to all who remember our matches ten years ago and the 'Old Uns' owe a great deal of their success to their excellent leadership.

"In the Walsall Swifts I should single out Yates for mention, a grand half-back, clever in tackling and always displaying excellent judgement in feeding his forwards. Poor fellow! He caught a severe cold on the field and died within a few days. That is how so many players collapse. They play in all sorts of weather during the most inclement part of the year; in the struggle they get tremendously hot and if there are not proper provisions for changing their clothes and having a bath, they run the most fearful risk.

"In my opinion the first attention of clubs should be directed to this matter and baths ought to be regarded as an indispensable part of the arrangements. I have known many a gallant and promising player die within a week of playing a match simply because of inattention to these precautions. It is folly almost amounting to crime to neglect this matter. But this is by the way.

"Another of the Swifts was Tapper, whom I specially remember on account of his scoring the goal in the memorable match in which we were defeated which I described to you last week. He was a very fast player and on that occasion, he seemed to be lying out waiting for 'snaps' and when he got the ball he went away with it at tremendous speed and scored. Then there was Alfred Jones, the Swifts' 'back' and for some time, captain. He was known as 'Jonah' and was a strong man in the team. If popularity is proved by nicknames, 'Jonah' must have been an immense favourite, for he was called also 'Jumbo' and the 'Returned Prodigal,' while mysterious references to Biblical subjects were as plentiful as they could be. Of course, being a 'Swift,' it was inevitable that someone should speak of Jonah being 'swallowed,' though on account of his size he was sometimes alluded to as the 'big fish' himself.

"I was rather irregular in playing for the Villa during this season, business calling me away; but I took part in the most important encounters, on several occasions journeying specially down from Scotland on purpose to do so. These were awkward times and I confess that often I felt as if I hardly had the requisite strength to play and do myself justice. I remember on one occasion travelling overnight from Ayr to Nottingham to play against Notts County. It was a bitterly cold morning and the journey down was far from pleasant. I knew no one in the town and felt miserable and weary. To add to my discomfort I had to wait several hours for the team to arrive from Birmingham and then in some extraordinary way I missed them altogether and was full of anxiety about their turning up at all. At last I hurried to the ground and there they all were – waiting for me.

"Of course, this is but a small incident and serves to show that, though the public may not know it, we are often forced to play in a very unfit state and are expected invariably to play our best. If we don't take every chance and put in a bit of brilliant play there are immediate murmurs that So-and-So is not up to form; and perhaps poor So-and-So has not been to bed all night and has been slowly freezing in a railway carriage for five or six hours beforehand.

"However, as I had been playing under considerable difficulties this season, I was presented with a testimonial of a very handsome character – a purse of sovereigns and a gold watch. Mr. W. M. Ellis, J.P., our esteemed President, made the presentation in a very complimentary speech and about 250 of my friends and friends of the Villa were present to hear him – Messrs. McGregor, W. B. Mason, George Ramsay and Jefferies among the number. As you know, I don't go in for speech-making to any great extent and really the proceedings were of such a character that I felt too strongly to be able to say more than a few words of thanks."

I suggested that Mr. Hunter should try and recall his remarks.

"No, no, I won't do that," he said. "They wouldn't look well in print – besides, they were so very few and short. But I certainly put my heart into what I said."

"Well," I said, remembering Archie's prowess, "it's a good job you weren't tempted to put your foot in it." He was pleased to smile at my small joke.

"This occurred," he continued, "in September 1881 and as I told you, I had only played on special occasions. I will now tell you something of the other Villa matches. The inter-association match – Birmingham and District versus London – provoked enormous interest and owing to previous defeats by the Metropolitan team a special effort was made by the local exponents of the game to win this match. It was played on 5th February and while our side was representative of the strength of the Midlands – all the important clubs but Wednesbury Old Athletics nominating a player – the London team was excellent. Everything was favourable to a good game but the weather and there were about 8,000 spectators in the grounds.

"The London captain, Woolaston, won the toss and elected to play with the wind at his back during the first half. I kicked the ball off – I was in my old position of centre forward with A. Brown for a partner – and

50

immediately there was a smart run into our territory. After a time my brother Andy and I managed to get up an attack and we took the ball right up to the goal-line and passed it to Brandrick (right-wing forward) who unfortunately missed the shot for goal. I had a slow shot at the goal directly afterwards and as the attempt to send the ball out was badly judged, Hawtrey only managed to save his goal by a quick punt, just as I charged him. This was followed by a capital run along the left wing by Keyser and it was only by Pank's plucky tackling that the ball was taken out of our territory.

"A hard scrimmage followed and then Bryan kicked out near the goal and the throw-in ended in the ball going clean over our lines. The kick from goal sent the ball to Johnson and in his company I ran it up the field, but Keyser returned it. After a bit of close passing we ran into the London goal, where Field (right wing) in attempting to send it out, put it over his own lines. The corner kick was judiciously placed by Johnson to Law, who was lying well out and was able to put in a high, well-judged shot. Bailey (half-back) succeeded in changing the course of the ball, but gave our side another corner kick and Andy placed the ball right in front of the London goal. Field received it and removed it with a fine kick to the end of the field, where Pank gave London their first corner. It was not long before our opponents got dangerously near our goal again and we had great difficulty to keep them from scoring; but at length the forwards drew the ball away and I got a good chance of scoring, but the ball was passed wide, greatly to the disappointment of our supporters. The Londoners then got a chance and Learoyd (forward) broke away with the ball at his toe and made for our goal with terrible speed, he centred the ball to Sparks and then our goalkeeper (Copley) had to use his hands and fortunately was equal to the occasion. The ball was not thrown out far, however and the London forwards surrounded the goal in a body. Our back division struggled manfully to turn the tide, but it was no good. The Londoners surrounded us and as Pank endeavoured to head the ball out it glanced off his shoulder and bounded through the goal.

"There was plenty of excitement, as you may imagine, but we were by no mans disheartened by the result, for we felt we were playing a pretty even game. On starting again I took the ball pretty near our opponents' goal, but several attempts on my part to score were frustrated.

"A slight accident happened a few minutes afterwards, Pank in taking the ball from Weston throwing him badly by charging low. Andy then made a couple of shots for goal, which were followed by one from myself, which was met by Hawtrey in a manner that evoked loud cheers from the spectators, who raised shouts of "Goal." I took the ball close in and shot from about five yards from goal. Hawtrey fell in stopping it and then Brown and Davis joined me in trying to force it through. We got it so far that it touched the chalk line, but then Hawtrey, who was still on the ground, managed to hit the ball with his hand to Field who immediately got it out of danger. What do you think of an exploit like that? Of course, we were sorry we had not scored, though we admired the way in which Hawtrey had baffled us; but we put on a spurt, being rather desperate and again got the ball well in our opponents' territory. Hawtrey still defended his goal magnificently and we failed to score.

"Next a curious thing happened. Johnson got clear away with the ball and had no one at last but the goalkeeper to elude. Then he suddenly lost his self-possession and did not sufficiently steady himself for the parting kick, and the ball, to our intense disgust, grazed the left-hand post. This was just before half-time was called and on changing ends we thought our chances of scoring much improved. So did the spectators, for they immediately began to crowd round our opponent's goal. But it was not such a certain matter and we soon found the leather dangerously near our own posts. Not long afterwards Andy met a mishap, his knee coming out; and though, with his usual pluck, he remained on the field, he was practically of little service. This seemed to dishearten us and some of the team did not play half so well as they had done in the first part of the game.

"However, the game continued to be exciting and once Andy got a chance, which his mishap could not prevent him from taking full advantage of and he centred the ball with a beautiful screw kick from about a foot off the goal line. Hawtrey was thoroughly surprised and only managed to touch the ball as it flew past his face on to Davis, who put it out again. Three corner kicks fell to us and from the last of these Keyser made off with the ball along the right wing and when nearing our goal he steered for the centre. Jones, by a quick dart, tried to stop him, but failed, and the goal was left without a back to defend it. Keyser's shot was rather weak, but he was so well supported that Copley could not get the ball away and in a short but sharp scrimmage it was forced through the goal. For the next fifteen minutes we played with the utmost determination, but there was no further scoring and thus the battle ended with a reverse for us – two goals to nothing.

"We had an unpleasant reverse a fortnight afterwards with Stafford Road, as I have before mentioned. The Villa up to the middle of February had an unbeaten record and we had met some of the best clubs and proved our superiority over them. It was, therefore, very hard lines to be defeated by Stafford Road, but the fact has to be stated. At half-time we had each scored a goal, and directly we had changed ends the Villa scored again. But while our opponents grew stronger and fresher as the game went on, our training told sadly upon us and we speedily became distressed. If we had been in our usual form we certainly could have avoided defeat, but Stafford Road scored two more goals, playing well. Unfortunately, this was the tie for the Cup and this reverse was fatal to our hopes of winning that trophy.

"It was just a month after this that we met the Wednesbury Old Athletics and beat them by six goals to none, much to their surprise, as I told you last week. I shall never forget that day and I ought to have mentioned that the entire proceeds amounted to over £360, which left over £100, after all expenses had been deducted, for the local charities. I can tell you also that so great was the interest taken in the game and so big was the excitement at Wednesbury, that at various times carrier pigeons were despatched with messages giving the result of the game up to the time the birds were flown.

"Then came the encounter with the Walsall Swifts and their unexpected win, our continual peppering at the goal being ineffectual. The 'glorious uncertainty' of the game was never more painfully exemplified – so far as we were concerned – than in this match. Lest I should appear to be prejudiced, I may quote what a local paper said of one of the players, who I will not now name: 'One of the half-backs, when tackling an opponent, over and over gain resorted to unfair means, using his hands in the most flagrant way and tripping frequently. He also displayed an irritability of temper that looked very bad on the field, on two occasions stopping the play and appealing to the umpires – once for a foul against Laws for tripping, when he himself was really the offender and another for the use of his hands when he had flung his arms round Davis.' It is no use denying that this was an ill-tempered match, one of the very few of the sort in which I ever took part. But the following week we were revenged, as you know and happily all ill-feeling afterwards disappeared, while personally I believe I was something of a favourite with the Walsall people.

"Our season concluded in April; the presentation to me took place in September and on the 24th of that month we resumed our contests, playing the first match of the season with the Wednesbury Strollers. This was not a very important match and as I took no part in it myself, I cannot say much about it. Copley, in stopping a ball from going through the posts, injured his left knee so seriously that he had to be carried off the field and Mr. Mason, who was then acting as secretary for the club, took his place. The Villa were defeated in this match by three to two.

"Our season was more properly opened the following week, when the Pollockshields Athletic met us at Perry Barr. Our antagonists had only just come to the front, having taken part in the final tie of the competition for the Scottish Association Challenge Cup for the previous season. However, we had no difficulty in disposing of them, although they had a good Queen's Park man, George Kerr, assisting them. A well-judged shot by Connell, one of the Pollockshields left wings, sent the ball through our goal early in the game; but after that the Scotchmen did not score again. We soon equalised matters and then had the play all our own way and in good time scored another two. Our opponents seemed to lose heart after this and partly on this account and partly owing to the dashing play of the Villa we gained a fourth goal within another five minutes. In about five minutes more Crossland added a fifth point and a sixth was added just before time was called. The match was not at all remarkable save for this rapid scoring.

"The following week we encountered the Walsall Swifts on our own ground, over three thousand people witnessing the contest. There were plenty of the Swifts' supporters among this lot and considerable feeling was shown by the supporters of each side during the progress of the game. In fact, not to mince matters, the proceedings were inclined to be rowdy. We gained two goals during the first half of the game, Brown and Whateley being credited with the winning shots. On changing ends each side tried desperately hard to score and the play was pretty rough; but the record remained the same and we were victors by two to one.

"The next week the Villa had the pleasure of meeting some more old friends, the Wednesbury Old Athletics, who came over to meet us with modified views on the subject of our capability. Business called me out of town that day and I was unable to be present. The contest was a close one and resulted in a draw, each side scoring three goals. Harry Simmonds bore off the principal honours in the fray, his back play being described as a grand exhibition and he received a hearty cheer as he left the field.

"I am sorry to say that I was again absent when the Villa met Notts Forest early in the following November. It was the second time that the two clubs had been opposed in the competition for the English Association Challenge Cup. In 1880 we had come off victorious, but Notts Forest was a formidable team and numbered some first-class players among its members. We were, therefore, by no means confident of coming off best and as details of the game prove, our men had to fight hard and put forth all their skill to win.

"The day was not favourable to the sport and heavy rain descended while the game was proceeding. Nothing, however, could damp the enthusiasm of the spectators, many of whom had journeyed from Nottingham to witness this struggle. A noticeable feature of this match was the large number of goals disallowed by Mr. Alcock, the referee, on the rule relating to 'off-side'. The ball was kicked through goal nine times and yet the score at the finish was only four goals for the Villa and one for the Forest. The ruling of the referee was a surprise to the spectators and the players on most of these occasions and provoked much comment and some hostility. However, let that pass. The Villa gained the day and that is enough for us to remember now.

"A match against Darwen a fortnight later resulted in a draw, but several disputes arose in the course of the game, which was of an acrimonious description. Darwen claimed to have won by a goal, but the Villa disputed the decision of the referee.

"Our team journeyed to Blackburn the following Monday to try issues with the Rovers. Three minutes after the start the Blackburn side scored, and within ten minutes a second point was added to their account. As soon as the ball had been kicked off from the centre the Rovers with a rush carried it into our territory and got it past the goalkeeper again; and within a minute they scored a fourth goal, to the frantic joy of the spectators. Vaughton scored a goal for the Villa after this and some hard play, characterised by desperate rushes and a few fierce scrimmages ensued. The Rovers, however, were irresistible and lowered our flag seven times, only two goals being placed to the Villa account. The team returned home thoroughly disappointed.

"In this match I was again prevented from taking part and you will begin to think that I am not telling you much of myself or of football triumphs. But I want to give you a little of the Villa history and not to be continually talking of my own exploits, or some of my old friends will think I am growing vain. Besides, it is not to be supposed that fortune was always on our side, and often enough we met better men than ourselves and sometimes we had to raise the cry of "bad luck." I think I may say, though, that we always tried to keep good-tempered and to accept our fate, whether good or ill, with a good grace. In December I was able to take part in the contest against Notts County, when a fast and exciting game was played. Five of our fist eleven were absent that day, while it was well known that the Notts representatives were in good form. We tried to keep our antagonists well on the defence, but they were the first to score, H. A. Cursham sending the ball whizzing through our goal in grand style. In fact this player carried off the honours of the match which ended in a draw, each side scoring two goals.

"On December 12th we played a most exciting game with Stoke-on-Trent, but when time was called each side had gained a goal and the match was left for decision the following week. The contest, I should explain, was in connection with the competition for the Birmingham Challenge Cup. On this second occasion the Villa came forth with honours and it was stated that the forwards – Crossland, Brown, Whateley, Davis, Vaughton and myself – had never played a finer game. We had the disadvantage and discomfort of playing in wretched weather, but our side were very determined and scored eight goals to our opponents' none. In the second half of the game we had to face a fearful storm, but still we played on and several beautiful runs were witnessed and just before the call of time I succeeded in scoring the eighth goal. The result was hailed with enthusiastic cheers and so ended our play for the year 1881."

Chapter 7

High Praise for Archie

"To sum up the season 1880-81," said Archie Hunter, "I should say that at this time Aston Villa was beginning to more than maintain its own as a first-class club. We had a great deal of hard luck during this period, it is true and the results scarcely attest our actual capacity at that time.

"As I have already explained, we were nearly winning both the Staffordshire and the Birmingham Cups at one time and in the latter tie we were beaten by a club altogether inferior to ourselves and inferior to other teams which we had met and thrashed during the season. However, it is our duty to take our luck as it comes and after all we were not disgraced – far from it. We won twenty-one matches, lost three and drew one and landed the Staffordshire Cup. No one can call that bad. Mr. J. C. Orr said of us at this period that our fortune was due 'to the ever-flowing spring of new and good men' who composed the team; while of myself he was pleased to say that I was 'probably the finest all-round player that ever stepped on to a football field'."

"Very high praise, Mr. Hunter! But do you consider you were at your best then?"

"Oh, no," said Archie. "My strongest seasons were from 1882 to 1885. Football all this time had been steadily advancing and excellent exponents of the game were rising up all over the Kingdom. This meant that we had superior teams to meet and had harder fights for victory every year; and unless a man could do better than he had done before he ran the risk of speedily being outclassed. At the beginning of 1882 the Villa took on fixtures with all the best teams in the country and very fine teams most of them were. It was something of an experience to play with them and it required all the strength we could muster and all the science we could display to play them on equal terms. That we did so and that from this period dates the beginning of a long and brilliant series of victories, is sufficient evidence that we must have continually improved upon our old form. I felt stronger and abler myself and I should certainly say that for those four years, 1882, 1883, 1884 and 1885, I never played a better game. You will be able to trace this as I tell you more of the matches in which I took part."

"I believe you were not playing much in the first part of the year 1882?" I asked.

"No, unfortunately, I was not," Archie replied, "My business still kept me in Scotland and I was not often present. But during this time some good matches were played and I should like to tell you something that the Villa accomplished. On January 7th we met Notts County at Nottingham – in fact, we played that club three times that season and each of the contests was of rather a sensational character. I travelled down from Scotland in order to take part in the second encounter, which ended in a draw, two goals each, one of which I scored. They came to Birmingham the next Saturday and then we thrashed them thoroughly by four goals to one. I again came down from Scotland to assist. As this was in the English Cup tie, it added to the importance of the victory.

"I ought to mention an extraordinary shot I made on the first of these occasions and if you don't mind I will give the account of it as described by another: 'After some tricky play with Arthur Brown and Oliver Whateley, Archie (who played on the left wing in conjunction with Eli Davis) got the ball fairly at his toe and the leathern orb went sailing away like a comet till it hit the pavilion behind the goal, quite fifty yards off. The Nottingham sightseers were never very generous in their plaudits for foreigners who visited them, but murmurs of astonishment at this display of strength were heard, while the little band of Brums who were congregated in one corner of the enclosure sent up a lusty shout, which must have been gratifying to the Villa eleven as they trotted off the field'."

"Well, how did you manage this, Mr. Hunter?"

"I can hardly explain it. I just got the ball right, you know and did my best with it."

"Your best was very effective," I said, "and I suppose you could say, with your favourite poet Shakespeare, it was done 'with a good leg and a good foot'?"

"Quite so," remarked Archie, evidently at home with this short quotation.

"The match with Notts on January 7th was in many ways memorable; and though the wind at times sadly interfered with our play and the forwards were not always able to pass with their usual accuracy, the ball being time after time thrown in and then blown out again, we accomplished some excellent runs and there was some grand display of dribbling on both sides. Harry Cursham, from Nottingham, was very strong and put in plenty of hard work. In fact, you can't say too much about him. He was a big player in those days and a great favourite in his district. He played right-wing forward and could always be depended upon for excellent runs – many of them of quite a sensational character. He was captain of Notts County and he and his brother Arthur, who died abroad, were the leading exponents of the game. Harry kept on playing until about 1888 and then retired and settled down in Nottingham. Many a splendid encounter we have had together and on this occasion he bore off some of the principal honours. I well remember how, when we were one goal to the good, he saw his opportunity and came away with the ball at a smart pace; then, when the ball was kicked out by Dawson, he took the corner, beautifully placed the ball and Arthur headed it through, amidst tumultuous cheers from the spectators. A bit of dribbling of my own all down the centre had elicited a good deal of applause not long before; and in short, it was a capital game all round.

"The following week the match at Perry Barr excited widespread and most intense interest. The tie had to be decided if possible and you can understand that the close and exciting nature of the two previous games had given rise to all sorts of speculations. It was not often that two first-class teams were found so evenly matched. The Nottingham club brought over a large number of friends and our own supporters rallied round us in a remarkable way, it being estimated that over ten thousand were present to witness this struggle – the final one as it turned out to be. I may remark that an old gentleman in the enclosure, who was probably too old to shout, had provided himself with a huge rattle, and every time the Villa gained a point he could be heard plying it with the greatest vigour. Then again, the scoring of a goal was followed by hats and caps being thrown into the air by our delighted well-wishers, who never seemed to trouble in the least whether or not they recovered their property. Fortunately, it was a dry day, though at times dull.

"At three o'clock I set the ball in motion and from that time every movement was closely watched by the excited multitude. It was not long before I got the chance of a capital header, but the ball bounced off the crossbar of the goal and over it. Time after time we besieged our opponents' fortress and one good chance was lost as the ball, out of a scrimmage, slowly trundled across the goalmouth and went over the line. But an opportunity was not long in coming and fortunately I was able to take advantage of it. From midfield I came down the centre with the ball at my toe and passed the half-backs; on the verge of goal the Notts back, Dobson, tried to arrest my progress, but I took him at the side, sent him to the ground and breasted the ball through goal, scoring the first point. We came near scoring twice afterwards very quickly and some clever passing by Vaughton and Davis gave the forwards another good chance and with a rush we carried the ball and some of those who endeavoured to kick it out, right through the goal.

"A pretty even contest followed and a run of mine evoked loud and continued cheers; the same compliment was paid to Cursham for a like performance a few minutes later. The play was very fast indeed and the Villa forwards were repeatedly applauded. 'The Villa' it was remarked, 'had seldom played a better game; the forwards worked together as one man and the back division did their duty well, Lee and Simmonds tackling in a splendid manner. For Nottingham H. and A. Cursham were far away the best of the forwards, but the play of the others did not sufficiently assist them. Moore at back and the Dolsons played in grand form and their splendid defence saved them from a more severe defeat.' As I have already told you we won the match by four goals to one."

"What was the next important fixture?" I asked.

"We met the Wednesbury 'Old Uns' twice and the first time, in January, I again came down from Ayr, travelling overnight, in order to play against them. Our opponents had the advantage of playing on their own ground and we were not in very good form that day, so that to the great disappointment of the host of Birmingham people who had followed us over we lost the match by four goals to two. I can't help thinking that some of the Villans were very funky that day, because the 'Old Uns' had a reputation for roughness which was not altogether undeserved.

"Did you ever feel timid?" I asked.

"Never," said Archie, decisively, "although I have seen plenty of rough play and even, at times, noticed a man lose his temper and use his strength furiously against another, I can't say that I ever felt afraid. Somehow I lost sight of all the possibility of danger in the hard work and the enjoyment of the game. We met the Wednesbury Old Athletics again in April, in the final tie for the Birmingham Cup and beat them by two goals to one. On the first of these occasions, however, we rather felt our misfortune, because it was the final tie in the Midlands in the competition for the English Association Cup. The first goal was scored for the Villa by Vaughton, who very cleverly got it past the goalkeeper. It was by a splendid long shot by Holden, the Wednesbury half-back, that the score was made even and there were some brilliant runs on both sides. I had a stroke of bad luck in the second part of the game, the ball from a throw-in being punted into goal by me and then it struck the bar and went out of play. But it's no good crying over spilt milk, is it?"

"But the match in April fully atoned for this, did it not?"

"Decidedly. It was a most important affair and the interest taken in it was simply immense. Besides, the game was not only well-contested, but it was of a very pleasant character. The Wednesbury men had been in strict training and as they had just before beaten the West Bromwich Albion it was expected they would again make a hard struggle to win. The match was in connection with the final tie of the Birmingham Cup.

"I travelled down specially from Scotland to take part in the encounter and kicked off. I was in good form and I may as well read to you an account of a bit of my play which I am proud to have placed to my credit. The writer says: 'The ball came out of a tussle to Archie and starting at full speed up the centre, he made the best run of the day. Passing Cliffe (half-back) with a neat bit of dodging he had a clear course before him and then about six yards from the goal he shot the ball low and straight for the goal, Kent, to the astonishment of all, caught it with his foot and saved his goal in splendid style with a kick to midfield.' That was rather a sensation for everybody, as you may well believe. Kent, the Wednesbury goalkeeper, was in grand form that day and did many marvellous and unexpected things in preventing us from scoring.

"Just before half-time I put on a short run from midfield and passed to Andy, the whole of the forwards closed up and forced the ball through goal amid a torrent of cheers. the score was now even, the 'Old Uns' having gained a point earlier in the game. In the second stage of the game we were somewhat favoured and approached our task with light hearts. When we scored our second goal the enthusiasm of the crowd really knew no bounds and the excitement only wore itself out with repeated demonstrations. Had it not been for the masterly manner in which Kent again and again kept the ball out of goal our score would have been increased five or six times. As it was, we were the winners of a grandly-contested game by two to one."

"Do you remember meeting the Wednesbury Strollers?"

"Well, I didn't take part in that match, which was played at the end of January; but I remember that it resulted in Clarke, our goalkeeper, breaking his leg. Apperley played with the Villa that day for the first time. I've not told you anything about him yet. He played half-back for four or five years and was very popular. He is now playing at the Cape as goalkeeper and is, I believe, quite a host in himself in that capacity. Apperley was an amusing fellow and once, after we had played a game in fearfully bad weather, the ground as thick as it could be, he went straight away in all his mud and had his portrait taken. He played pretty well against the Strollers, but Whateley carried off the honours that day, scoring twice in splendid style.

"After that came the match with Sheffield Town, on February 4th. In this contest the Sheffielders' goalkeeper, Mallinson, distinguished himself and but for him the Villa would simply have smothered their opponents. Harvey, for the Villa, played remarkably well as 'back' and Vaughton, Whateley and Brown worked well together. The Villa won by three goals to nil. Exactly the same result attended their match against Derby the next week and the Villans followed this up by beating Saltley College by two goals to none a week later. The match with Darwen, on March 4th, resulted in a tie, each side scoring two goals. The feature of the day was the obtaining of a very hard goal by the Villa. Vaughton shot the ball, but Duxbury, the Darwen goalkeeper, was too quick and threw out; Brian whizzed it back and again Duxbury fisted it away; then Whateley obtained possession and one of his quick, low shots sent the ball through the posts."

"You took no part in this match, I suppose?"

"No. I was still away and though I should have liked to meet the Blackburn Rovers the following week, when the Villa lost by one to four, I was unable to be present. I understand that the principal feature of the match was the fine dash and combination of the winners' forwards and Hargreaves, in particular, played a grand game. Some of the Villa team, it was remarked, seemed slow and indolent at the beginning of the game and hence, perhaps, the signal defeat they experienced.

"On March 20th an interesting encounter took place between the Villa and the Walsall Swifts in the semi-final tie for the Birmingham Cup. Nearly ten thousand people witnessed the match, many of whom had come from the Black Country. There was much uncertainty as to how the game would end and hence there was no lack of excitement during the whole of the proceedings. The Villa did not start playing in the best form, but afterwards greatly improved. Ugly rushes and awkward scrimmages were the order of the day. Eli Davis had a particularly fine run with the leather and shot the ball in well; it was low on the ground and it seemed to many of the players that Hobson (the Swifts goalkeeper) did not get on to the ball until it was through goal. The score, however, on appeal, was not allowed. When the Villa scored their first goal a tremendous cheer was sent up and amid the din several carrier pigeons were seen to wing their flight from the brakes round the field, carrying the tidings of the Swifts' downfall to Walsall. No other goal was scored by either side and the Villa were thus winners by one to nil.

"We beat the Glasgow Rangers the following week by three goals to two. This was the first time the Rangers had been to Birmingham and their great reputation naturally made many wonder how our team would fare against them. In the first half of the game the English rules were observed and in the second half the Scotch. Ten minutes before half-time Danvers got the leather in midfield from McNeil and crossing to the left wing ran down quickly. Nearing goal he turned sharply and getting the ball fairly on his left foot sent in a splendid side shot. Copley, our goalkeeper was taken quite by surprise and the ball, with great force, struck him on the breast and bounded through the goal. On sides being changed the Scotchmen were two goals to the good. Curiously enough, during the second part of the game, when the Scotch rules were being enforced, the Villa scored all the advantages and eventually gained three goals; and as the Rangers did not score again, the home team were victorious. The result was very heartily received by the spectators, who, in spite of a very inclement day, had mustered in good force.

"A very big beating awaited the Heart of Midlothian, whom we met at Edinburgh and defeated by six goals to one. But an equally sad fate awaited us the following Monday, when the Glasgow Rangers beat us on their own ground by seven to one.

"On April 24th we again met the Wednesbury Old Athletics, this match being in connection with the efforts of the Birmingham and District Association to establish a charity fund by offering a handsome Cup for annual competition. This was the third time we had met our old rivals this season. The day was unfavourable and the spectators few; but the game was a pretty one and ended in our favour by two goals to nil. In this match Anderson was hurt, a collision early in the game cutting his left eye badly.

"The Villa, being the winning team, had now to meet the Walsall Swifts in the final tie and the game was played off on May 6th. Happily the day was favourable and the gate amounted to over £200. All round the enclosure the spectators ranged in an unbroken, deep line, whilst the stands were packed to their utmost capabilities. The match itself was a most enjoyable one, though it was evident that both sides were feeling the result of the strain of a long and heavy season. The Swifts played a dashing game, but during the first half the Villa scored twice and in the second half they took the lead, played magnificently together and gained four more goals, two of which were disallowed. The Swifts scored one, and thus the Villa terminated a good season by winning the Charity Cup by four goals to one.

"Talking of the Mayor of Birmingham Charity Cup leads me to think of Mr. Joseph Cofield, the late respected secretary of the Association, who was very highly esteemed by all players and deserves special mention. He devoted a great deal of time to fostering the game of football and spared no efforts in encouraging players. I never knew a more popular man. He was presented with a silver tea-service for his long and valued services to the Association and also with a purse of money. The latter he returned to the Association for the purpose of founding a Charity Cup, which at first it was decided to call by the name of the donor. But Mr. Cofield, among other attributes, possessed that of modesty and by his special desire it was called the Mayor of Birmingham's Charity Cup.

"It was a very severe blow to us all when he died and perhaps the more so as his death was sudden and unexpected. He caught a severe cold and never recovered. It was his custom to attend all the matches he could and he accompanied us whenever we went out of town to play. On these occasions no member of the team was allowed to want for anything. Mr. Cofield was always ready to do everything he could to make the journey happy and pleasant and to fit the players for their work. He was also one of the chief supporters of the Aston Lower Grounds Cricket and Football Club. I never knew him as a football player, although he had played in his younger days. In him the Association lost a most devoted servant and every one of us a sincere and trusted friend. It took the heart out of some of us when we knew we should never grasp his hand again, never see his cheery face, never have him with us at our gatherings, never – but there! He is gone and we shall not look upon his like again."

Chapter 8

Good Times for the Villa

"We are now coming to exciting times," said Archie Hunter, as I sat down, pencil in hand, to note the chief points in his eventful history. "The latter part of 1882 was very successful and during this time the local popularity of the Villa grew very great.

"We started with a splendid win against Stafford Road on September 16th, in a match for the benefit of the Birchfield Harriers Club. It had not been expected that I should play that day, but almost at the last moment I found I could come down from Scotland and I wasn't going to lose the opportunity. Down I came, therefore, rather to the disappointment of Crossland, who was to have played in my place. Clarke, who had met with an accident the previous season, as I have before explained, was able to come down and keep goal for us and we were a very strong team altogether. On the other side there were plenty of good men, but early in the game it was seen that we were more than equal to them. We scored in fifteen minutes and other points were added in quick succession. A smart shot from Richards, one of the Stafford Road forwards, caused our goalkeeper to use his hands. The play was very fast and the Stafford Road tried their utmost to turn the tide; but they failed and we ultimately won by eight goals to nil. It was a very plucky game on the part of our opponents, but the whole of the Villa players proved themselves in very good form that day."

"I think you said that this was only a friendly match?"

"Yes. So was the next match, which happened to be with our old opponents, Notts County. This was played at Perry Barr and I was not present. I may as well tell you, however, what was thought of the club at this time and I will read the report of a local critic. 'Our premier club,' he said, 'promises this year to be stronger than ever.' The back division has certainly improved on that of last year, while, with Archie Hunter back again and Roberts, the new man in the forward division, the attacking strength is very great.' Crossland was put in the centre while I was away, but on this occasion he did not play a good game throughout – in fact, in the second half of the game he was quite off colour. The Notts team were a very strong lot as usual, and were the superiors of the Villa in height and weight. The match was disastrous for the Villa, for while they missed several easy chances of scoring in the first part of the game, their opponents had all the luck on their side, in addition to their well-known scientific ability.

"There is no doubt that the defeat of the Villa by two to one was a disappointment to everyone in Birmingham. Cursham's first goal is described as being a remarkable stroke of luck, but at half-time the scores were level. A few minutes before time A. W. Cursham scored a very good goal for his side and the Villa were unable to equalise matters. I should like to say this about Notts County; they were an excellent team and played a good, scientific game, but were rather given to using their physical strength to the disadvantage of their opponents. They pressed hard and shot well and I have already told you of the exploits of the brothers Cursham."

"What was your next important match?"

"Well the Villa met the Sheffield Wednesday the following week and won by six goals to one. We had met this club some weeks before and had been defeated by one goal to nil; so that you see this was in the nature of retrievement. There was nothing very particular in the play at either match, but I am reminded at this point of an old Sheffield Wednesday player who deserves to be mentioned. I refer to William Mosforth, 'Billy', as he was called, one of the oldest international players and one of the first to play the Association game. He was noted for his fine dribbling displays and for many years continued to be one of the speediest players we met. We liked to meet him, too, because he was a capital fellow and always gave his opponents a fair chance. He was very strong, but never used his weight unfairly."

Here I thought it a fitting opportunity to murmur the words of the bard:

O, it is excellent
To have a giant's strength; but it is tyrannous
to use it like a giant;

but Archie took no notice.

"He was as popular at Glasgow as he was at Sheffield and as much liked by the Scotchmen as their own players. He must have been playing seventeen or eighteen years altogether – a remarkable time for a first-class player to last."

I was strongly tempted again to indulge in a quotation from the 'divine William' – "A tanner will last you nine year," as the gravedigger said to Hamlet – but on second thoughts I refrained.

"What about the match, Mr. Hunter?" I asked.

"Oh, nothing much. Eli Davis, Andy and Vaughton bore off the principal honours and the greater part of the game was played in the Sheffielders' territory. There was a much better game the next week in the English Cup tie, when we met the Walsall Swifts, a big crowd assembling to watch the contest."

"Were you present this time?"

"Oh, yes. I was there and we played our strongest team. I captained the Villa and Clarke was in his place as goalkeeper. Andy, Vaughton, Brown, Roberts, Eli Davis, Simmonds (backs) and Bryan, Anderson and Harvey (half-backs) made up the team. The Swifts seemed to be less strong than in previous seasons and we did not find it very difficult to beat them, the scores being: Villa four goals and Swifts one. Our passing that day was favourably commented on and I remember coming away from our goal with the ball at my toe, passing the Swifts' forwards and then leaving Vaughton to send in a fine shot, which was altogether too much for Hobson."

"The Villa now felt fairly started for the season, I suppose?"

"Exactly so and very well started too. Of course we weren't invincible and when some of us went over to Sheffield the following week, as

Birmingham representatives, this was proved. The Birmingham team on that occasion was captained by Tom Bryan, who belonged to the Wednesbury Strollers. The Strollers were at that time a first-class team and Tom was one of the first to play Association football in this neighbourhood. It was, therefore, only right that he should be chosen captain. He had had for comrades at Wednesbury, Alfred Harvey and Eli Davis, who afterwards joined Villa. We journeyed to Sheffield and Mr. Cofield went with us, acting as our umpire. At this match Mosforth played a splendid game – in my opinion the best game of the day. The ground was heavy and we had to work very hard. Yates, who is now dead, I am sorry to say, and Bryan played well, but we were defeated by five to two. It is rather a curious circumstance that every time we went to Sheffield we failed to win. Of course, the victory of the home team was remarkably well received, as it deserved to be."

"What were the features of the play?"

"Well, we all put in some good shots, but the Sheffield backs were very hard to pass and we could not score. The state of the ground told very severely upon a tall player like myself. I can only say that though defeated we were not disgraced."

"That almost goes without saying," I remarked.

"We met the Walsall team in the tie for the Staffordshire Association Cup early in November and a very hard, tight struggle it was. The wind was blowing very strong and prevented accurate play and we came very near losing the day once or twice. Bird, who was the best forward in the Walsall team acquitted himself with the greatest credit and was a tower of strength to his side. It was simply by determination that we pulled the match out of the fire. I had some difficulty in getting the team to play in combination, but at last I succeeded and we eventually gained the victory by two to one. The captain of the Swifts was Newman (three-quarter back) who was a very persevering, if not a very brilliant player. He organised his team well and we always found Walsall Town hard to beat.

"There was one good thing about the Villa, as everybody knows, I

71

think, who ever saw us play. We had the power of making up our minds to win and when that determination was once upon us the other side had got some hard work to do. I can recall many occasions when our chances were looking hopeless and our supporters were already giving up the prospects as lost, when suddenly we would pull ourselves together, make a dash and bring the balance on the right side. This was the result of personal hard work and good combination and it was this capacity of ours which served to make the Villa matches interesting. No matter how badly we began, nobody could tell but that we should redeem ourselves before the call of time. On the other hand, some of our seeming certainties were surprisingly belied.

"Take the match we played only the week after the one I have just described. We met Darwen and quite expected to beat them. The Darwen Club was strong at that time, but just beginning to drop away. To our surprise and to the surprise of over six thousand spectators, we lost by two goals to one. Darwen scored first; then Roberts scored for us. Then Darwen scored again and, well, we didn't. There is only this to say in extenuation: the Villa played a mixed team, part of our team having to go to Sutton Coldfield for the Birmingham Cup tie which resulted, I am pleased to say, in a win for our side by five goals to nil.

"But to return to the English Cup tie. We encountered the Wednesbury Old Athletics again on November 20th. They were now beginning to decline and since our famous victory over them they had never been the power they were in the football world. Many of the players were changed too and I don't think the new men were so good as the old. At all events we had no difficulty in beating them – in short, we swamped them, that's the fact. The match was witnessed by a large number of spectators. The play was fast and rough at times. I put in several good shots early in the game, but the Athletics drew first blood. We rallied after this and I led the forwards on and some capital runs followed. We gradually got the upper hand and at the call of time we were four goals to their one.

"But all this time I have been obliged to tell you of comparatively small affairs. I must now give you an account of a big encounter in which I took part as captain of the Birmingham and District Association against Lancashire Association. Tom Bryan had retired from active play and now umpired for us. I had been elected to succeed him and got together the best team I could. This was very necessary, for the Lancashire Association was very strong indeed and we knew we should have all our work cut out to beat them. I am quite convinced that the best team won – though that team was not ours. The weather was very favourable and an exciting match resulted in a victory for the Lancashire side by two goals to one. The representatives of the Red Rose were very strong, the eleven comprising six of the 'Scotch contingent' who had done so much to promote the dribbling game in the locality. Our picked team would have been stronger if the Wednesbury Old Athletics had contributed a man or two, but owing to another engagement of some importance that club required all its strength and could not place any of its players at our disposal. Our valued goalkeeper, Clarke, was also absent and we were forced to put Keay in his place, a matter which occasioned us some regret as he did not play up to form.

"The first part of the game was very even, though with the wind in their favour the Lancashire men had a little the better of us. The back play of our opponents was very fine and one of the principal features of the game was the splendid tackling of Hugh McIntyre. Harvey and Yates, on our side, did some fine work and the former saved the goal twice after Keay had missed badly. The forwards did their best and we had rather hard lines in not scoring, as we continued to press our opponents very hard. The first goal was scored in less than a minute from the kick-off, our goalkeeper being completely baffled. This woke us up and we commenced to make a desperate attack upon the Lancashire citadel. The play was very hot indeed, the passing and returns arousing the greatest excitement. I had three splendid close shots in quick succession all in the right direction; from one the ball struck the goal post and the other two were got hold of by the Lancashire backs, so no score was obtained. Hacking, of the Blackburn Rovers, who kept goal for the Lancashire side, had plenty of hard work and did it marvellously well. The wonder was how he got at the ball, but he did and cleared his goal time after time.

"The second goal for Lancashire was gained soon after half-time and had Keay displayed a little agility it would have been saved. But we got a chance later on, for Hargreaves and Steele made way up the left wing, Apperley took the ball from them and passed to Andy who made off with it along the line. He centred to me and I put in a hard one, but Hacking, who was playing a magnificent game, shied the ball out. I followed up again and this time got out of Hacking's reach and with a full kick shot the ball clean through the posts at a terrific speed. We now thought we could draw, for there was another twenty minutes left for play. But it was rapidly growing dark and the Lancashire men wisely massed round their goal and played strictly on the defensive. I had a bit of bad luck, for one of my shots would assuredly have scored had not the ball just touched the back of Warburton's foot with the result that it just spun over the line close to the goal. This was practically our last chance and at the call of time we were beaten by two to one."

"Then you consider that bad luck partly accounted for your defeat?"

"Well, I shouldn't make too great a point of that. I don't want to say that whenever we didn't win it was bad luck, because that would convey a wrong impression. I repeat that the more powerful of the two teams won, but the result might have been different if we had had our own goalkeeper and one or two of the Wednesbury Old Athletics with us. It was a stubborn contest and all things considered I think we did well."

"Quite so. And now what was your next match in this eventful year?"

"Our next match was against the Derby Midland, in the Birmingham Association Cup tie. We took the field with only nine men, Whateley and Davis not having arrived. It was rather an unequal match and we did not anticipate any particular difficulty with our opponents. This led us into a little danger at first, for they played up remarkably well at the beginning of the game and got unpleasantly close to our goal. However, we couldn't allow this to continue and carried the ball into the Derby territory and I scored the first point with a fast, low shot which Haynes failed to meet. The game finished in our favour by four to nil.

"By-the-way, there was a queer fellow in the Derby Midland Club whom I call to mind at this moment and he was accountable for a very laughable scene upon the field on one occasion. I forget which match it was, for we met the team several times, but at one of them he played a most eccentric game by making perfectly mad and reckless rushes at me when I had the ball. It was easy enough to avoid him and every time he came near I just dodged him and he went sprawling on the ground. He got up again game enough and continued this curious behaviour, repeating it whenever he had the opportunity; but he did it once too often and at last, after an ugly fall, he lay still and I took the ball half the length of the field without being stopped at all. I have never been able to account for the man's tactics to this day, but I know they provoked the greatest merriment to the spectators. He must have appeared highly ridiculous, especially as he never had the ghost of a chance of accomplishing anything."

"Do you think he was mad?"

"Well, his rushes at me might be described as such; that's all I can say. The following week – the second week in December, the weather became very wintery and rather changed our plans.

"It was our intention to play two matches on December 11th – one a Staffordshire Cup tie with the West Bromwich Albion and the other a home-and-home match with Notts Forest. If that plan had been adhered to we should have sent a strong team to Nottingham and strengthened the second eleven with one or two of the first eleven to meet the Albion at Perry Barr. The Nottingham match was postponed owing to a heavy fall of snow on the previous Friday and consequently, Davis, Vaughton, Clarke and myself remained at liberty to strengthen the team to meet the Albion. And well it was that we could do so, for I verily believe we should have been thrown out of the competition if our team had been weaker than it was. It was a very stiff struggle indeed. The Albion were just coming to the front and were by no means to be despised. They had young, strong players among them who practised assiduously and they played up very pluckily and made the work warm for us. We only succeeded in making a draw – three goals each – and during the progress of the game I had to make several important changes in the positions of the team. At half-time the Albion were a score ahead, but in the second half I kicked the third goal and equalised matters.

"We met again a fortnight later – December 23rd – and then what do you think happened? The Albion won and we were thrown out of the competition after all. Bad for us, wasn't it? Only one goal was scored and the other side scored it. It is true that some of our regular players were absent – Vaughton, Clarke, Anderson and Brown among the rest – but we didn't anticipate the defeat.

"In the interval – that is, the previous week – we had met and beaten Stoke, a club against which I always played well. I can't account for it, but such things do happen. I had some splendid runs and scored frequently. Not so very long before, this Potteries team had been very high indeed on the list of dribbling clubs and they still had some good players among them – Ringland, Brownfield and Boddington were particularly prominent. Brownfield was a capital athlete altogether and had won fame as a sprint runner. We were expected to win and win we did in thorough style by five to one, three of the goals being placed to my own account. The ground was in a wretched state and once I fell just as I had a sure goal in hand.

"This, I think, brings me to the end of the list for the year 1882 – a year memorable to me for many pleasant matches and much progress and a year which I believe all footballers remember as the date of the real beginning of our greatest fame as a club.

Chapter 9

A Memorable Season

"We began the year 1883," said Archie Hunter, "by playing the Aston Unity, who were once a strong club, but at this time declining. It was the misfortune of this club that when it had good players it could not keep them and our own team was often reinforced by the best men from the Unity.

"There were reasons for this, of course. Money may have had something to do with it, but perhaps it would be going to the truth of the matter to say that after all, everybody likes to be on the winning side. The Villa had, by now, proved itself most successful and all the best players in the town were anxious to be admitted to its ranks. Nothing succeeds like success, you know and it is the same in football as in everything else."

"But the Unity was still able to play a good game, wasn't it?"

"Of course it was. Though we fairly over-matched the team they put in the field, they were by no means contemptible opponents. Tom Butler, poor fellow! who lost his eyesight, was gone, and Benson was captain in his place. A rattling good player the Unity had in Harry Pallett, who has since become even better known in the cricket field and whose bowling last season was so sensational. He was a splendid half-back, very clever with the ball and his height assisted him."

"Is it not unusual for football players to go to the cricket field afterwards?"

"Well, not altogether. I have known men very fond of both the games and good exponents of both, too. In addition to Pallett, another example might be found in Gunn, the Nottingham crack, who is also a footballer. I also met him in this season of which we are now speaking, as I shall tell you later on."

"To return to the match, then, Mr. Hunter. What were its principal features?"

"Its principal feature was that the Villa proved to be rapidly improving on its old form and that the Unity, which had originally been able to beat us, was falling back. The Unity played a plucky game, but we were altogether too much for them and we won by three goals to nil. The first goal, gained by Vaughton, was a splendid one; but before the second was scored Apperley fell heavily in charging and was obliged to leave the field, play being suspended for a short time. The third goal was kicked by myself.

"The following week we had a runaway match with the Small Heath Swifts and established a record. Our opponents were a young team, but had entered bravely for the Birmingham and District Cup and it fell to their lot to encounter us first. Well, we were in very good trim and practically the Swifts could do nothing to oppose us. I don't know how many goals I kicked myself on this occasion, for I speedily lost all count. Probably I gained a dozen or so. Anyhow, at the end of the play the score stood – Villa 21 goals, and Small Heath Swifts none! It was at this match that a humourist fetched our goalkeeper a chair to sit down upon, as he had nothing to do. But Copley hated inaction and once, being tired of standing between the posts and never getting a chance of using his feet, he came up the centre of the field and as the ball was shot from our opponents' goal he struck it back again with his fist. I may add that from that return we scored. But then we could have scored from anything. It was a glorious day – for the winners. At half-time ten goals had been placed to our credit and in the second half we scored eleven."

"Was there any brilliant play?"

"No, none in particular. We were too busy sending the ball between the posts. This match was played on January 13th and the following week the Villans met their old friends the Derby Midland again. The captain of the team was Harry Evans, a popular player and a good all-round athlete. He gained Association honours, but does not play now. He is the superintendent at the College Street Station in Glasgow. You see this time the order of things was reversed and Scotland imported an Englishman, but not as a player. When I met Harry he was playing centre-forward and if all the Derby Midland had been as good as he was, we should not have won so easily. I did not play in the match now referred to, but the Derby team was not very powerful and there was a half-back among them who was one of the wildest and most mad-headed players I ever heard of in my life. He rushed all over the field, but never did anything very important. This match was played at Perry Barr and ended in a win for the Villa by four goals to none. The Derby had a bit of bad luck in one of their players, Chaplin twisting his knee and he was not able to play again.

"The next Saturday I took part in a very hard struggle against Walsall Town, in the English Cup tie. Speculation had been rife for a long time as to the result of this match. Additional interest was given to the encounter by the fact that the winners would be able to enter into the final tie for the national trophy. A writer at the time observed:- 'On past reputation of course the Villa were far and away the better team and if that were the chief means of gauging the capabilities of football elevens, few would have hesitated to foretell the result of the match. But football, like cricket, is a game of glorious uncertainty and though an eleven may be known to contain within itself material vastly superior to that of another organisation, those who know anything about what are really the conditions which prove the greatest factors in the result of a game, base their prognostications altogether on the latest form displayed and would therefore prefer a team whose capabilities were inferior, but who were in fettle, to one whose members had the ability to play a better game, but had allowed that ability to deteriorate.

"'In a somewhat limited degree that was the position of the two contending clubs. The Villa at the beginning of the season were playing in brilliant form, but from one cause or another up till the previous Saturday their play for the past six weeks was anything but satisfactory. On the other hand,' continued the writer, 'the Walsall Town eleven have been of late more and more to the front and though their defeat of the

Blackburn Rovers was at first thought to be greatly owing to good luck, since that they have shown plainly that they were a vastly improved combination by thrashing the famous Sheffield Wednesday.' We knew all about this and had gone into special training a fortnight before and by the time that the match had to be played there were plenty of people who were unable to make up their minds which side would be most likely to win.

"'It was a fearfully bad day and the ground at Perry Barr was never in a worse state. This was all the worse for us, for the Walsall team were used to mud, but we were lovers of fair weather. The ground was described by an eye-witness as being 'a perfect quagmire of treacherous bog-like mud, while for fully fifteen yards outside the goals there was not a blade of grass to be seen and between the bare patch of the upper goal and the middle of the field the water lay in three large pools, extending more than half across the field'."

"I suppose you didn't care for the prospect much?"

"Not much," said Archie. "Still the game had to be played and we were there to play it out, both sides putting their strongest men into the field. When the game commenced it had ceased to rain and the sun sent down blinding rays upon the sheet of water in which we were wading about. We lost the toss and had to play uphill, facing the sun, buffeted by a gusty wind and having to pilot the ball through the thickest part of the pools. My goodness! it was a match. We had every reason to fear the worst and our consternation was increased when the ball, on being kicked off, was taken down the right wing and shot through our goal – all within a minute of starting. It's a marvel we had the heart to go on. But fate was not against us after all. After the first ten minutes we settled down to hard work and determined to win. You know what that meant."

"Certainly. You might almost say in the words of the song:-
Along the line the signal ran,
England expects that every Villan
This day will do his duty.
Isn't that it?"

"Yes, that expresses it. Of course we had a terrible task before us. The water stopped the ball dead and a clean kick was no good. The player had to lift the ball out with a spoon kick and probably before he emerged from his bath someone had made off with the leather. The spectators were mightily amused, of course, on such occasions, but it was no fun to us to kick a ball as heavy as lead and to feel the water clinging round our ankles. We equalised matters before half-time, Vaughton getting a good goal and a second goal was obtained by Arthur Brown, who was in the centre with me. The Walsall did not score again and thus we won, in spite of everything which had looked so unpromising at the outset. Among the Walsall team that day was Sam Reynolds, a determined player, excellent back, good tackler and splendid kick. He has stuck to the club and is still playing. Another Walsall Town man is Cox, the Villa captain this year, my own successor, who began to play in the first team in 1883, as far as I can remember. He played well, too and early distinguished himself and wishing to get on still faster, he joined the Villa a year or two later. He played full back then, as now."

"It is a curious coincidence, Mr. Hunter, for the old Villa captain to have met with the present Villa captain in this way."

"Yes, it is. If you would like my opinion of Cox, it is that he is one of the best full backs in the country at the present time. He is a grand kick, places the ball well to his forwards, tackles his opponents in the most masterly way and is equally remarkable in his defence. In short, he is a brilliant player and combines excellent judgement with his personal skill. Under him the Villa should go on well and I only hope that his duties as captain won't interfere with his own powers of play."

"What do you mean by that?"

"I am speaking from experience and I mean that a man finds it diffi-cult to do his best work while he has got to look after a team, pull the men together, guide them, see that they don't get scattered and make certain of their taking every advantage, as it comes. I can tell you it is a hard job and there is the danger that in looking after the organisation of his forces the captain will be unable to play a good game himself. I don't think the difficulties of captaining are fully understood and it is very seldom that any allowance is made for the skipper's extra duties. Sometimes it is terribly hard work to get the team to combine well and it is the captain's first duty to look after this before making individual exertions. And while he is shouting out his orders and keeping an eye upon his men, what wonder if he is apt to neglect a chance or fail to see it? It is on account of these possibilities that I said I hoped the captain of the Villa team would not be spoilt as a player while holding the high and responsible office he does."

"And now for your next match, Mr. Hunter."

"It was against the Blackburn Rovers, who, you know, were an almost invincible team at this time, and who afterwards obtained celebrity by winning the English Cup three times in succession. By the way, would you like a list of the English Cup winners?"

"Yes, I think it would be very interesting."

"Well then, here it is up to 1887.

1872	London Wanderers
1873	London Wanderers
1874	Oxford University
1875	Royal Engineers
1876	London Wanderers
1877	London Wanderers
1878	London Wanderers

(Presented to the Association by the Wanderers in 1878).

1879	Old Etonians
1880	Clapham Rovers
1881	Old Carthusians
1882	Old Etonians
1883	Blackburn Olympic
1884	Blackburn Rovers
1885	Blackburn Rovers
1886	Blackburn Rovers
1887	Aston Villa

"Our encounter with the Blackburn team took place on their ground and we took over with us Albert Brown, whose first season it was with the Villa and he played a most serviceable game. He is, as you doubtless are aware, still playing for the Villa and is considered to be one of the cleverest members of the team. He came from the Aston Unity and was the brother of Arthur Brown, my old centre-forward comrade.

"The match was fairly exciting, the tactics of the Rovers at the opening of the game being remarkably good. They scored a quarter of an hour from the start, Hugh McIntyre shooting the ball through goal. We equalised matters before half-time and directly after play was resumed Jimmy Brown, of the Rovers, lowered our flag again. But again we got level and in good time; and playing up in true form we began to press our opponents very hard. Then Albert Brown came to the front and sent the ball spinning through the posts for the third time. The Rovers felt called upon to make an effort and only by the cleverness of Mason, our goalkeeper, were we saved several times. Jimmy Brown, however, equalised matters again and now the intensist excitement prevailed, for we only had a few minutes to keep on playing. Fortunately, we were equal to the emergency and Olly Whateley kicked the winning goal just before the whistle blew.

"I regard this as one of our best matches and our win by four to three advanced us another step in local popularity. Jimmy Brown, whom I have mentioned, was a good centre-forward and had won international honours. After McIntyre – who also distinguished himself by his good play that day – he captained the team. Brown was very fast, a splendid dribbler, and a sure shot. The two Hargreaves, though not playing that day, were noted members of the Blackburn team and the elder of them was for some time captain, but had to retire on account of an injury to his leg. Among our own men who deserve special mention for their play against the Rovers is Vaughton; and Mason also worked well at goal.

"On February 10th we met the Aston Unity at the Lower Grounds, Aston, in connection with the Birmingham Association Challenge Cup. It was not much of a match and we had an easy victory. The Unity were very unfortunate about this time and had lost most of their best men. During the first-half we scored seven goals to nil and when time was called we were sixteen to none. Of these Brown scored ten goals – his dodging being simply superb on this occasion – Dawson three, Davis one, Whateley one and Vaughton one.

"But a big and brilliant victory was awaiting the Birmingham and District team, of which I was elected captain, the next week. We met a representative London team at Aston and beat them by three to one."

"Will you tell me some of the incidents of the match?"

"Yes. There were about ten thousand people present, the day being a very favourable one. About a quarter of an hour from time some of the spectators tried to get inside the enclosure and the consequence was that a general rush was made by the crowd to the play line, the players for the remainder of the game being hampered very considerably. The match was exciting from beginning to end. The Londoners scored first, but shortly before half-time, I equalised matters by sending the ball through the posts with a swift low shot which was too much for Bates, the goalkeeper. In the second part of the game I headed a fine combined run and gave our opponents some warm work. Then Brown took the ball up to Whateley and the latter started at sprinting pace and passed it prettily to George Holden, who had a straight unopposed run. The Old Athletics' representative passed the leather to me and I popped it into the charge of Bates, who could only interpose his body and as the ball rebounded Howard Vaughton was waiting for it and got it safely through. Loud cheers greeted the performance. The performance was repeated with trifling variations not long afterwards and it was generally remarked that the Birmingham forwards exhibited beautiful combination. I have mentioned George Holden and I should like to say of him that he was a very strong player and was of immense service to his club on the right wing. He and Arthur James used to play a remarkably good game together.

"But the most exciting match of the season was, I think, that which followed when we met Notts County in the English Cup tie. You will remember that the Villa and Notts always had a hard struggle and this was not at all an exception to the rule. The match about which I am going to tell you bears an historic name and is called 'the long-armed match' to this day.

"Why is that?"

"Because Harry Cursham with his long arm accomplished something rather unusual. It was this way. The tug of war was very severe, as everybody knew it would be. So great was the interest taken in the match that eight thousand people went over from Birmingham to Nottingham to witness it. Cursham started the ball for Notts and if it had not been for Apperley would have scored right away. Gunn, the famous cricketer, was one of the left wings and distinguished himself by a grand run ending in a goal – the fourth for Notts. Perhaps he never played better in a football match than he did that day and time after time he was wildly cheered for his exploits. I scored the first goal about half an hour after the start, but at half-time, through Gunn's instrumentality, the score was equal.

"In the second half Cursham got the leather through our posts and increased our ardour in endeavouring to win. Later on Cursham scored again and the record was now three to one. Working hard we succeeded in scoring our second goal, Whateley being the medium, but at this critical point the people broke in and seriously interfered with the play. Some temporary stands had broken down and there was plenty of excitement from that cause, in addition to what was provoked by the game. Well, we scored again and matters were equal once more. Then came Gunn with a tremendous rush and scored again, Notts thus claiming to win by four to three.

"But we claimed also to have scored a fourth goal, in spite of the decision of the referee, for the following reason. Howard Vaughton had charged the goalkeeper and we believed, had got the ball through goal. The goalkeeper could not reach it as it was flying through; nevertheless it was fisted out and we had evidence to show that it was by means of Cursham's long arm that the trick was done. In the excitement of the moment, of course, it was impossible to tell exactly from our own observation if this was the case, but independent witnesses were ready to prove that it was. So I lodged a protest against Cursham and claimed that the match was a draw. We went to London with several witnesses to prove that the ball had been fisted out of goal by some other player than the goalkeeper; but as the referee declared he had seen nothing of this, the decision went against us.

"This was an unlucky match for me altogether. As I was going back to the station the immense crowd surged around me and eagerly inquired the result of the protest. When I got to the station I discovered that someone had taken the opportunity of relieving me of my watch and chain – the watch which had been presented to me by the Villa and the chain which had been given to me by my Ayrshire friends. This ended the day's disasters. Nevertheless, the 'long-armed match' saw some good work done. Andy and Olly Whateley on the right wing had matters nearly all their own way in the second part of the game and scored their two goals in quick succession. As for Gunn's runs, they are famous to this day.

"But now let me show you a little humorous effort of ours, which may be introduced at this point. We played the Wednesbury Old Athletics this season – a season of which I shall have more to tell you next week and in particular must give you an account of our trip to the Highlands – and we issued the following bill, printed in red and black with plenty of Old English type in it. It was very effective and may raise a smile:-

Oyez! Oyez! Oyez!

Ye Royale

GAME OF FOOTBALL

Be it known

To eache and everie of you that ye Righte Merrie gathering for ye propere enjoyment of A Grande Game will be holden atte Aston, in ye Towne of Byrmingham, on ye day as followeth:-

SATURDAY, APRIL YE 7th, 1883,

Atte 3.30 of ye clock, and finish at 5.

An it please ye to favoure ye Committee appoynt, for ye propere management of ye said entertainment wyth your presence and that of ye faire ladyes and gentlemen your fryendes, ye are requeste to cum earlie. Ye Gallante Players will eache excel in skilful parts.

For ye Town of Wednesbury:-

Mastere	Kent	Mastere	George Holden
„	Moon	„	Grocutt
„	Nicholls	„	Wood
„	Hodgkiss	„	Morley
„	John Holden	„	Tonks
		„	Woodcock

For ye Village of Aston:-

Mastere	Mason	Mastere	Archie Hunter
„	Simmonds	„	Brown
„	Bryan	„	Whateley
„	Apperley	„	Davis
„	Anderson	„	Vaughton
		„	A. Hunter

And be it known to everie that Masteres George Holden, Brown, Vaughton and Whateley have honourably raised ye banner of merrie England in ye joust of ye World.

Ye Knights in command will be masteres Moon and Archie Hunter, who will take due notice of ye guide counsels of Masteres Campbell Orr and Durban.

Mastere Crump will sweetly discourse ye signals of ye Game, and to him will atte all times obedience by paid.

Wines and Cakes and other dainties may be obtayned at a faire rate.

Chapter 10

Chiefly About a Famous Tour

"The Villa played a match in the snow," said Archie Hunter, "against Wrexham. Although it was the middle of March the weather was very severe and scientific play was almost impossible. Our team won by six goals to nil, but I can not give you any particulars of the play, as I was away. The Villa was also minus the services of Whateley, who had gone to Sheffield the same day to play in the match of England versus Scotland. On March 17th, however, I was back again and playing 'back' too, instead of centre-forward as I usually did."

"How did you like your new position, Mr. Hunter?"

"Not so well as the old one," replied Archie, "The paper said that I was 'in every way a fitting companion for Simmonds, but I did not feel quite at home. It was so long since I had played 'back' that I felt out of form, especially so far as powerful kicking went. However, we more than held our own against our opponents – St. George's – and beat them by four to one. Eli Davis was loudly cheered in an early part of the game for a magnificent run finishing with a long shot at goal, which all but scored. The Dragons made some good runs too, but we were equal to them all through the game.

"And now we come to an eventful time which all the old members of the Villa Club look back upon with the greatest interest. On Saturday, March 24th, we travelled to Glasgow to meet the Glasgow Rangers. This was like going back to the old home for me and we determined to spend a few days in bonny Scotland. And we had a good warm time of it, too. On the Saturday we met the Rangers, but had a somewhat unexpected defeat by four goals to one. It was a pleasant game and if some of us had not been worn out with the journey we should probably have given a better account of ourselves. During the following week we played no fewer than six other matches with such clubs as Arbroath, Dundee Harps, Airdrieonians and Perth St. Johnson. We lost the Airdrieonians match, but, as far as I can recollect, won the rest. The field we played on against Airdrie was like a hard road and did not suit us at all."

"I suppose you journeyed about the country when not engaged in playing?"

"Of course we did," said Archie with brightening eyes. "But here! You can read all about it in this diary, kept by Apperley."

So saying, he put into my hands the following account of the Highland trip.

Thursday, April 10th, 10.30 p.m. – we, a merry little party of fourteen, comprising Messrs. Alf Harvey, Tom Riddell, Jim Benson, Fred Dawson, George Price, Charlie Apperley, Arthur and Albert Brown, Olly Whateley, Archie Hunter, Eli Davis, McGregor, Jeffries and Mason, started from New Street Station by the Scotch mail, bound for the Land o' Cakes. Nap, of course, was the game worth living for and soon the familiar cry of 'Pass Three' betokened the exhilarating presence of the great railway monopolist. At Crewe a combined attack was made on that gastronomic goal – the hamper, the determined efforts of the team eventually lowering its colours.

Good Friday – 'Ere Carlisle was reached, Somnolence began to exert its soothing influence, upon which a certain prominent half-back, Apperley, came to the rescue of the general hilarity. A concert in a railway saloon was a decided novelty. "Fling dull care away," cried his delighted club mates, amidst the inspiriting strains of the whistle on the Carlisle trolley, so 'puffing Billy' had to dance attendance on puffing Charlie.

Glasgow, 9.30 a.m. – The Gerrard Street Unfortunate opened his chapter of accidents by splitting the knee of his go-to-meeting pants in his anxiety to first tread Scottish soil (?) – i.e., the Central platform. Dinner at the Central Hotel was followed by the unexpected, but none the less welcome, appearance of the Camlachie Distillery Friend, who accompanied us to Balloch, about a two hours' journey and situated at the foot of Loch Lomond. We started from Glasgow at 11 o'clock and after a wash and snack at the Balloch Hotel, being of divided minds, forsook that combination for which we are generally famed. One party took to the water, while the remainder drove over to Luss, the seat of the Colquhouns (*Vide* 'Rob Roy'). The way to the house led through a magnificent carriage drive some three miles long and the deer could be seen in plenty from our vehicle in the surrounding park. After having returned and enjoyed dinner, we regretfully saw the Friend off. At 7.30 p.m. a couple or so of the staid ones retired to bed, but several more of us who had not done enough work for the day, found our way to Alexandria, the return journey (luckily!) being also successfully negotiated.

Saturday – Three of the team tried the piscatorial (?) pursuit of crab-catching (to say nothing of eye-blacking) at six o'clock in the morning on Loch Lomond. The water was too deep for 'Big Ben' who accordingly tried the shallows, minus shoes and stockings (what a calf he has got, to be sure!) Bird-nesting and rabbit-hunting was followed by breakfast at 8.30, after we lazy ones had been called downstairs. We next journeyed to the scene of action. The visit several of us paid to Messrs. Denney and Sons' shipbuilding yard proved a very interesting feature of Saturday's programme. Of the match I intend to say next to nothing, more especially as I was one of the twenty-two players. McKinnon, the international, was the champion of the afternoon, his runs and centres being a perfect treat to witness. The splendid defence of Alf Harvey and Tommy Riddell was admired greatly, while we had terrible hard lines in not once breaking through the miraculous opposition offered by the Scotch backs. Two of the goals scored against us we got for them, while, had the game been played on a larger ground than Bonhead, the peculiarities of which the home team are thoroughly acquainted with, we should certainly not have left the field without making a much closer thing of it. Still, the winners played a dashing, honest game and I should be the last to endeavour to slur over the brilliance of their well-earned victory. The dinner which followed the match was a most enjoyable affair, the teams fraternising together in happy style. A warm sprint only just enabled us to catch the Glasgow train. A wet at the celebrated Athole Arms and we took the 9.20 p.m. to Callander, arriving there about half-past eleven. We patronised the Dreadnought Hotel, a lately-added wing of which we occupied for the night.

Sunday – Four of the early birds tried a 'constitutional'. The ragged highland tramp washing himself at the spring formed an exceedingly romantic picture, at least so my club-mates thought, until the cheery voice of our trusty guide, philosopher and friend dispelled the illusion by the jocular remark, "Look at his Dumbarton!" (The noble army of outsiders who object to being sat on by such unintelligible pleasantries as these will obtain full explanation on application to the noted Summer Lane Drapery Depot. – N.B. Ladies need not apply.)

"After breakfast we drove to Lochs Lubaig and Erne. Mount Erne was scaled by several of the more enterprising ones. A muchly-prized pipe, owned by one famous half-back, was broken accidentally by his now equally-famous partner. "Offside, Alf" came down upon the waiters at the bottom laden with ammunition and great was the slaughter thereof. Milk with bread and cheese at Loch Erne Hotel led on to a fine drive through Rob Roy McGregor's own particular hunting ground. After dinner several of us visited the celebrated glen, bridge and waterfall near Callander.

"Returning, a most mysterious adventure befell my club-fellows. It appears they manage these little things better in Scotland than we do here, for in this case, at all events, 'followers were allow-ow-owed,' and a high old time they had of it too. The apple and meat pies, to say nothing of the Scotch whiskey, were greatly relished and A. B. richly deserved a vote of thanks for his warm discovery. The 'false alarm' created a general exit via the garden wall, but all came off right afterwards. Two of us who had not been sharers in the delightful little romance paid a visit later on to this Gaelic paradise, likewise returning home in triumph laden with a couple of pies (about two feet across!), for

91

the sake of which we all risked the terrors of nightmare by commencing on a second supper.

Monday – At 8.30 a.m. we started off in two brakes for the Trossachs. Lochs Vennacher, Achway and Katrine were in turn scanned and admired. Rob Roy's grave near to the Pass of the Trossachs was an object of great interest to all of us (Mac in tears!). The 'Sad and Silent One' (Nemesis, we thank ye for those words) could not resist the temptation of a plunge into the classic waters of Loch Katrine, while Olly and Alf, not to be beaten, tried a header from the boat-house. I have not hitherto spoken of the grand scenery, of which we were all enthusiastic admirers. The respected descendant of the notorious Highland Chieftain whom Sir Walter Scott immortalised years ago was fairly in his element. His intimate knowledge of all the neighbourhood through which we journeyed made him an invaluable 'illuminator' of the trip. To him every stone and tiny rivulet we passed possessed some historical charm. The beauteous lakes caused him to bubble over with pardonable patriotism and lo, his arms opened to the rugged grandeur or the towering mountain peaks that hemmed us in on all sides. Birmingham lads born and bred caught the contagion and losing sight for the time of their individuality, willingly – nay, joyously – surrendered themselves to the witchery of Bonnie Scotland's glorious landscapes.

The return journey was made remarkable by a most sensational escapade. When within some forty of fifty yards of the Trossachs Hotel the rear brake came rather unexpectedly to grief, owing to the collapse of the hame. Horses, brake and seven prominent members of the team went down the steep bank together (some eight or nine feet) en route for the brook, which was a like distance across. 'Quick march' was the order of the day and the alacrity displayed by the occupants was astonishing even to their more fortunate comrades, who knew what they were capable of. 'Belger's plague,' in the act of leaping, was jerked by a short lurch of the carriage clean over the stream on to the opposite side, where, as he happened to drop on 'a soft place,' no further harm was done. Dawson, in bolting, turned a beautiful catherine wheel, dropping on his back, upon which he was promptly sat on by the Daisy-cutter. Freddy, forgetting the compulsory state of affairs, in an indignant tone, asked "where are you coming to?". Apperley, who sat on the box, was unable with anything like safety to get clear off, so with as much Micawberesque philosophy as he could muster on so short a notice, waited for something to turn up. That something was the brake, which decidedly 'turned up' in the brook, depositing poor Charlie under the wheels and far nearer than was pleasant to the hoofs of the struggling quadrupeds. One of the wheels passing over the half-back's ankle rendering him hors de combat. Luckily, no more harm was done than a badly sprained limb. Archie was to the fore, carrying the sufferer pick-a-back to the hotel. After Apperley had been attended to a gig was chartered to convey the spilled to Callander, which was reached at 3 p.m. Going on from there to Stirling we spent three or four hours there, leaving poor Charlie in the saloon with the remains of the apple pie.

At 8.30 p.m. we left Stirling for Birmingham. We were all tired out and slept most of the way back, arriving home about 6.30 on Tuesday morning, after the jolliest club outing we have ever spent. Booze was very little patronised, for we were moving about too much. One of the milk vendors, in order to meet the clamorous demand for more, was publicly charged by some of our members with filling the empty can with water and palming the same on thirsty Villans as the genuine Simon Pure. We are all in good health and spirits (even Charlie may get right in time) and mean pulling off for the third year the Charity Cup. Should auld acquaintance be forgot? Why, certainly not.

"It seems, then, that you filled up your time well," I remarked.

"Yes," said Archie, laughing at the recollection "and we spent the money too. I remember that Teddy Lee, Olly Whateley and myself were staying at a hotel and at the end of our time we found that we had forgotten to save enough cash to pay for the journey home. Of course, our Glasgow friends very readily put us all right and I only mention this to show that we had thoroughly given ourselves up to enjoyment, without any thought of the future.

"When we got home the next Saturday we played the Rangers on our own ground and although they were a hard lot to beat, we beat them by two goals to one. It was an exciting match and over six thousand spectators were present to witness it. We had had to make several changes in our team and Apperley and Joe Simmonds did not play. Considering the strength of our opponents, our busy week and the reverse we had already suffered at their hands, we were prepared for defeat. So were our local supporters. But it's the unexpected that happens, you know. Fortunately, the weather was splendid and everything was favourable to a good passing game. So we set to work. Losing the toss we had to play uphill, but soon began sending in hot shots. Tremendous cheering greeted us when we scored the first goal. The Scotchmen played a defensive game, but once or twice we came so near scoring that they were forced to come out more boldly, and the result was that after besieging our citadel for some time they were rewarded with a goal. On resuming, after half-time, Vaughton and Whateley had a splendid run and a corner was gained. This was well placed by Davis, Brown headed it into goal and it went through out of the scrimmage. The Rangers tried hard to equalise matters, but failed. Perhaps the most noteworthy feature of the game was Arthur Brown's play at half-back. He was always in his position, but when I wanted him he dashed forward and contributed in the most effective manner to our success.

"The 1882-3 season was now coming to an end. On April 14th we encountered Stoke on their own ground. Though our opponents played up with spirit, they really had no chance against the Villa and it was evident to us that as a club they were rapidly declining. The old players were stale and the new ones not up to form. At the end of the game their banner bore the sad device – Villa 9, Stoke 1.

"The following week we had a grand game with Walsall Town in connection with the Mayor of Birmingham's Charity Cup. Both sides were strongly represented and the fight was a hard one. Cox played in this match and from a return of his the Walsall forwards made off with the ball and after a combined run succeeded in drawing first blood. Another dashing run was made by the Walsall forwards and Bradbury, the Walsall centre forward, fairly passed Simmonds, our back; but Apperley (half-back) rushed up just in time and saved what seemed to be an almost certain score. The Walsall wing men showed such good form that they caused us a lot of trouble; and our shots were repelled so well that it seemed as if we should never get the leather between the posts. A second point to the Walsall made our supporters rather downcast and I had to do my utmost to get the Villa to play together. At length Andy with a low one popped the ball through and not long afterwards Whateley scored for us again. Matters were now equal and remained so until half-time. We attacked the Walsall stronghold and from a centre of Eli Davis's one of the Walsall men headed the ball through his own goal, registering another point for us. But again the score was equalised by Walsall and now the excitement was intense. We worked with a will and on both sides some really fine play was shown. But Whateley, the daisy-cutter, with a low shot got the ball past the goalkeeper and the match was won. The game was truly said to be one of the very best ever played in Birmingham.

"The final tie for the Mayor of Birmingham's Charity Cup was played on May 12th, between the Villa and the Walsall Swifts at the Aston Lower Grounds. Heavy rain during the week had rendered the ground sodden and the attendance of spectators was not so large as we could have wished, considering the cause to be served. However, over eight thousand were there. Invitations had been sent by the Association to the Mayors and Corporations of Birmingham and Walsall and both these bodies were represented. The two clubs, as you are now well aware, were old rivals, but on this occasion we were particularly successful and carried all before us.

"After only two minutes' play Brown delivered a close shot direct into the Walsall goalkeeper's hands, but before Hobson had time to fling it out Whateley, following up with a rush, sent the ball and its custodian several feet through the posts, securing the first goal for us. This rather nonplussed the Swifts and we took advantage of their discomfiture.

Scarcely had the ball been again set rolling than Whateley got hold of it and passed it to me on the left. I sent it flying towards the Walsall goal and Vaughton rushing up in the nick of time drove it grandly through the Walsall posts. Thus our second point was gained within five minutes of the start of the game. Only another two minutes intervened before we scored again and the delighted spectators applauded long and heartily. The Swifts seemed to have little ardour after this and only with an effort recovered their pluck. They played chiefly on the defensive; 'A solitary gleam of hope,' said a writer, in giving an account of this match, 'rewarded the efforts of the defenders, for the Villa captain slipping down, Higgins got the ball and sent it into mid-field. The too cautious tactics of the Swifts which led them to crowd too much in their own lines prevented them from reaping any advantage from the opportunity and Brown on the Villa right, by a piece of remarkably skilful dodging took the ball back through the opposing forces and passing it dexterously to Eli Davis at the mouth of the Swifts' goal, the latter, with a sharp oblique shot, lowered the visitors' colours for the fourth time in a quarter of an hour, amid intense excitement.'

"It was a very brilliant bit of play," continues Archie, "and our luck, once again, never deserted us. At the call of half-time we were five goals to the good and at the end of the game the score was Villa 8, Swifts 0."

"And what became of the Cup, Mr. Hunter?"

"We won it every season but one," Archie replied, "and that one season we drew twice with the Walsall Swifts. Then it was decided by the Association to engrave the names of both clubs upon the plate."

And as I looked round Archie Hunter's cosy little parlour I saw plenty of evidence in the shape of framed addresses that he had done his share in winning the Cup for his team.

Chapter 11

The 1883-84 Season

An esteemed correspondent writes us as follows:-

'Triumphs of the Football Field' have been progressing capitally; far better than at first I thought them likely to do. I have been perusing them with palpitating heart, bloodshot eyes and aching bones on the first opportunity each week – Friday night, which is not my custom, for I generally put the paper by until I have had a good rest – say Sunday. I am so eager to hear the 'old hoss' (Archie) jawing, that I cannot brook delay. I have no fault to find, nor suggestion to make. An old footballer is always gratified by any scraps of information regarding the 'big guns' whom he has oft seen perform. Archie has not lost sight of that. When a noted player has entered the 'triumph field,' he (Archie) has thrown a few morsels to us poor dogs of sixpennyites. Let him remember, the more of these scraps the better the book.

One thing has struck me in the course of these 'essences' – Archie could not see just how everything happened (whilst he was busy playing) like a spectator could. For instance, in the match 'twixt Aston Villa and Walsall Swifts, at the Lower Grounds, he mentions about a Walsall back (Ashwell, I think – Ash something; he was not the regular Walsall back) appealing idly and vexatiously to the referee. I refer to the cup tie – the sensational one, wherein the Swifts unexpectedly (especially to themselves) won! (the week after the Villa licked Old Athletic six to a handless frying-pan). This is what happened. I stood within a few feet (while a respectable man who was with me can swear to the truth being as I tell you) and the match was in a very critical state for the Villa, it standing 1 to 0 against them, whilst they had shot their bolt to all appearances. Well, Ashwell was a very tall, thin chap, with spindle-like shanks. He was a new hand, an unknown quantity – but he played very steadily (without the least roughness), reliably and with more skill than the temper of one of the Villa men could quietly allow. Time was becoming short, every chance led to a desperate, knacker's-yard-like scramble. Ashwell secured the ball well in the corner of the right wing of his own goal (from whence a centre would have been just the thing for the Villa); Sammy Law bundled into him like an electrified bundle of old rags and bones to dispossess him of the ball, a desperate bit of work ensuing betwixt these two.

What Sammy Law was renowned for was his desperate, energetic tackling; but this time he failed to get the ball when there was a good chance at a critical time, which, with the excitement, rage and surprise at the unexpected state of the game, proved too much for his self-control momentarily, for as Ashwell (having 'done' him) lifted his long spindle leg to give the ball one good parting kick toward the Villa goal, Sammy Law out-manœuvred him in a helpless position (as far as fair play is concerned) at the back of him, kicked him viciously, nastily, on the shin. Ashwell, as I have said, was a large man, chiefly bone. Had he retaliated, what would have become of little Law I shudder to think; but the Walsall man did not do so. As far as I could judge, he was a fair, right-minded chap. He walked up to the referee (some sixty yards away) and being unable to get any satisfaction from that official, seized Sammy Law by the shoulders, shaking him and apparently demanding an explanation. Thereupon Eli Davis bared his leg and exhibited a large and fine assortment of knightly wounds in various tints of purple, blue and gray, to Ashwell, thereby eliciting thunders of applause from the thousands of spectators. That was all the satisfaction Mr. Ashwell got.

Archie says, in the match 'twixt London and Birmingham, the ball was put through again by the Londoners after a bit of a scrimmage. Archie was too far away to see just how it was. There was no scrimmage. It was the softest thing I ever saw. A London man and a kid came out with the ball down the centre, all opposition passed except Copley, the Birmingham goalkeeper. The London chaps were clever at shooting, knowing which, Copley, rather than wait for a red hot plum pudding in the smash, chose to lose his head and to run out of goal at the man. Of course the man, when Copley was on him, passed the ball to the kid and the kid lost no time in putting it through the empty goal. I was standing behind the goal. Just then Law raced up, too late; but never shall I forget the long, fixed stare of utter disgust with which he regarded Copley. But I have seen Copley display the highest of goalkeeping – as against Queen's Park at Perry Barr.

In the match against Walsall Town of which Archie speaks this week, the first goal was scored from the left wing (Bird I think), not from the right. It was done before the Villa were quite aware that the game had commenced in earnest. It was a rare match for the spectators; as the players dashed into the pools of water and struggled each one to have his own blooming way in ordering the ball about, we could see huge sprays of water answering each kick and baptising the kicker and his foes indiscriminately.

"Falls were frequent; indeed, we (the specs.) thought somebody would be drowned. No doubt it was unpleasant for the players, but had they been lookers-on, merely, would not they have laughed as heartily as we specs? Towards the close – the score standing Villa 2 Walsall 1 – the Walsall chaps (all hurry and excitement), tried to judge it as unfairly in taking a free kick close at goal (there was great rivalry 'twixt the teams at that time). Thereupon Archie uplifted his voice, "No! let us have it out fair." He could not have said anything better (unless he had said "fairly"). It had more effect than any amount of appeals would have had.

"The letter may be correct," said Archie Hunter, "and it gives me an opportunity of making a necessary remark as to this narrative. I should have a very wonderful memory, indeed, if I remembered the details of every match in which I played; and though I think I am usually correct in my statements, yet if sometimes I say we won a match by four to three when it should have been five to four, perhaps the reader will make some allowance."

"I have no doubt that this common-sense view has been taken already," I said. "And now for some account of the 1883-84 season."

"The 1883-84 season was a remarkably prosperous one," said Archie, "and I will here give you a summary of what the Villa accomplished before proceeding to details. We played forty matches, won twenty-seven, lost eleven, drew two and obtained 128 goals against fifty-eight scored against us. The average had been slightly higher the previous season (1882-83), when we played thirty-nine matches, won twenty-seven, lost eight, drew four, and obtained 160 goals against only fifty-five scored against us. These figures show a remarkable increase on the preceding years."

"Have you the figures for those years?"

"Oh yes, if you would like to have them. Perhaps they will be interesting for the purposes of comparison.

OUR RECORD IS AS FOLLOWS:-

Season 1878-79

Matches played 18

Won 12

Ties 2

Lost 4

Goals obtained 45

Goals lost .15

Season 1879-80

Matches played 26

Won 20

Ties 4

Lost 2

Goals obtained 89

Goals lost .32

Season 1880-81

Matches played 24

Won 21

Lost 3

Goals obtained 93

Goals lost .23

Season 1881-82
Matches played 30
Won 17
Ties 7
Lost 6
Goals obtained 86
Goals lost .54

"So you see in the last two seasons (1882-3 and 1883-4) we had made big strides and you will see as time goes on that we gained more victories every year up to the end of 1887. The 1883-4 season is one, however, to which we look back with pride and our secretary, in his report issued in May, took occasion to remark that:- 'Though your committee have again to record defeat in the competition for the National Trophy, they can point you to this season's victories over some of the most renowned teams in the Kingdom, notably: Blackburn Rovers (English Cup holders, 1884), Blackburn Olympic (English Cup holders, 1883), Notts County, Oxford University, Dumbarton, Edinburgh University, Darwen, &c. and further would remind you that on only two occasions, when opposed by the Queen's Park, has Aston Villa been beaten while playing the full strength of the Cup team.

"'Locally, the reputation of your club has not only been sustained, but enhanced, by winning, for the third consecutive year, the Birmingham and District Challenge Cup, thus entitling you to its complete and absolute ownership, a result of which we may well feel proud. In addition, we may congratulate you on again holding that magnificent work of art, the Mayor's Charity Cup, thereby indisputably proving your right to the foremost position in football circles in this district. We feel proud that, whilst attaining these objects, we have in some degree aided in the higher and nobler one of supporting a movement for assisting our sick and injured fellow-townsmen.'"

"Who was your secretary then?" I asked.

"Mr. Samuel Richardson," Archie replied; "a schoolmaster by profession, who took an enormous interest in football and was a good judge of the game. He devoted a great deal of time to committee work and was highly esteemed. Mr. Mason was secretary before him and when I first joined the Villa, Mr. Charlie Midgley was the secretary and did the club at that time a great deal of service. The first balance-sheet of the club with which I am acquainted was drawn up by him and this is a copy of it."

Archie here produced one of the relics of the club which he treasures.

"Your will see," continued the Villa captain, glancing at the sheet, "that mention is made of a Villa Cricket Club. I suppose you don't know that I used to be a bit of a cricketer myself?"

"No, I never heard that you played cricket," I said.

"Well, it is a fact," said Archie. "The Aston Villa Cricket Club claimed me as a member and I played in their matches. But cricket did not succeed like football at Perry Barr and in a short time the cricket club collapsed. I more frequently played with a club connected with a local firm's warehouse and called the Arcadians. Both as a bowler and a batter I obtained some recognition. I bowled round-arm and sent the ball in very fast. In a match played against Edgbaston a gentleman offered a pair of batting gloves for the highest score made that day and I won the prize with a record of twenty-three runs. So, you see, I gained honours even on the cricket field."

"And how do you like the game compared with football?"

"Oh, it is a good game, but not quite exciting enough. I like cricket immensely when I have the bat or the ball in my hand, but I don't like the long wait to go in and bat and the weary interval of doing nothing if you don't have a long innings. No, give me football for excitement and plenty to do and always something to employ everybody on the field? But we shall never get to the season's matches if we are not quick," Archie added and thereupon began an account of a contest with the Blackburn Olympic.

"At the end of the previous season," said Archie, "we had been fortunate enough to defeat the Blackburn Olympic by five goals to one. As you know, the Olympic were that year particularly strong and our great victory is to be accounted for that we played upon our own ground and that the hard training they had been undergoing had begun to have its effect upon them by the time we met them. But in September, 1883, we went to Blackburn to play the return and by this time the Olympic had picked up again. It was a very hard match indeed and in the end we were defeated by two goals to one. We did not send over our strongest team, I ought to say, while the Cup-holders were in splendid form and the captain, Jack Hunter, played a grand game. The second part of the game was full of excitement and we made a desperate effort to avoid the defeat, but could not succeed in scoring.

"The season having thus opened, football became all the rage in the Midlands and I never remember the enthusiasm being greater. A topical writer of the time said:- 'Football is the game of the day. Before it cricket pales and croquet hides it insipid head; quoits and bowls become elderly and suburban and even lawn tennis is a feeble pastime of sunshine and flirtation. The vigorous and hearty football has virtually kicked all other games out of the field. Not only do teams travel hundreds of miles to play matches, but enthusiasts travel hundreds of miles to see them do it. From Glasgow to London will believers journey and doubtless from Dan to Beersheba should football permeate Palestine.

"'Special reporters take football in hand and columns are written about it daily. Decidedly, too, the sport is gaining favour with the fair sex. At a late encounter in these parts the ladies stood five deep in the enclosure and evinced the most lively interest in the tremendous 'kick-up' that was going on. The dear creatures have mastered the slang, too and talk occult football lingo gaily and glibly.

"'Now the game is not without its dangers, as we know. Few players are there who cannot show honourable traces of wounds received in action in the field. It may be that as the pugnacious German student is glorified in the eyes of his beloved by what might be termed 'prime cuts' received in student duels, so the British footballer is adorned and beautified, even, by ebony and cerulean contusions. Why not, then, a Ladies' Football Ambulance Society, with its able and beauteous members always on duty on the football field, clad in the sweetest and most coquettish of uniforms and alert to minister to the afflicted gladiators. We will say that Algernon, young, handsome, brawny, but sadly knocked about, is borne unconscious from the field of glory and suffering shins. The blushing and beautiful Belinda is by his side and promptly ministers to his sufferings. I see it all – the old, old story, so hackneyed yet ever so sweetly new –

She loved him for the dangers he had passed,

And he loved her that she did pity them.'

"This paragraph, at all events, gives an indication of the interest manifested in the game. I can remember when we first started the Villa that it was difficult to get reports of matches in any newspaper and our captain or secretary had to write them himself. But that is all altered now and in the Midlands the Villa assisted materially in the change. Whenever we left town to play a match big crowds went over with us and when we returned big crowds were waiting to meet us. Football reports were eagerly read and during the last ten years nearly all the cheap popular papers devoting special attention to this branch of sport have been started."

"And now to return to the matches again," I suggested, after this digression.

"A match which excited a great deal of attention," said Archie, "was that with Sheffield Town, in October. I was not able to be present myself and J. Simmonds, Arthur Brown and Roberts were among the absentees. Consequently the Villa had to play some of their second team men and it was at first thought that we should suffer a reverse, as the Sheffielders were strongly represented. As it happened, however, there was not the slightest cause for anxiety and our team simply crushed the Blades, winning by fourteen goals to nil. Although the Villa only played with ten men for some time they scored twice and afterwards they had matters all their own way.

"Some new names are introduced by this match, that of the goalkeeper, Archie Vale, being perhaps best remembered. Then there was little Jones, a promising member of the team, who played for some time with his fellow countryman, Roberts. He had to return to Wales on account of business, and I have not since heard of him. Foster, who played back with Jones against Sheffield, was a tall and strongly-built young fellow, who did good service for the team. Lodge, who played with Eli Davis on the left wing, was a very good youngster, but scarcely realised expectations and never came out as we thought at one time he was likely to do. He is now in America. I ought to say of the Sheffield team that they were a gentlemanly set of fellows, who played football purely out of love for the game and did not go in for very severe training. They were capable of making a very fair display, but when matched against a team like the Villa they were altogether out-classed.

"The following week we had the pleasure of again meeting the Blackburn Olympic, who came down to Birmingham. A great deal of the interest which this visit excited was due to the fact that the Olympic were the first provincial club to win the English Association Cup. Our previous victory had been taken as a proof, at the time, that we were superior to the Cup holders; then our defeat by the team had given the other side a chance of asserting that they were more than our equals. Consequently, the present encounter was looked upon as being to some extent decisive so far as our rival claims went. The weather was good, it was a splendid October day and the spectators turned up in good number.

"The Olympic having won the toss, I had to start the ball up-hill and against a slight breeze. Our attack was considered strong, but the Olympic defence was very fine. After a considerable amount of spirited play on both sides and some dashing runs, the Olympics drew first blood. The game then became very fast and we pulled ourselves together and attacked the Blackburn citadel with resolution. Up to half-time, however, nothing more resulted.

"After the interval we again settled down to work and pressed the Cup holders very hard, time after time taking the ball into their territory. They resisted for some time, but Whateley secured the downfall of their colours from a centre of Vaughton's, our local supporters, of course, cheering vociferously. Again we assumed the aggressive and enjoyed one or two exciting runs. At last I got possession of the ball and succeeded in eluding the Blackburn backs. I passed to Whateley, but he did not see an opening and quickly returned the leather to me. I got the ball at my toe and by a well-aimed shot gave the Villa the lead. There was a perfect uproar of applause at this prospect of victory. The game was most stubbornly contested to the end, but we ultimately left the field victorious by three goals to two.

"The victory created the greatest enthusiasm in the town and after so well-played a game from which we had emerged with flying colours, our hopes of future honours were high. Jack Hunter again played brilliantly and the reverse his team experienced was a great disappointment to him. But our victory added to our reputation as a club and I went home feeling that a good day's work had been done."

Chapter 12

A Busy Season and It's Result

"The 1883-4 season," said Archie Hunter, "was what I call a very busy one and to the end of the year we had an almost unbroken record of success. Meeting Walsall Town again at Perry Barr, on October 20th, we beat them by four to nil, the Walsall team playing up gamely, however and not going down without a struggle. There were some splendid exhibitions of passing in the course of the afternoon, but otherwise the game was like many others that we had played with this team.

"In our encounter with Queen's Park, the following Thursday, however, there were a few exciting incidents. This was the third visit of the famous Scotch dribbling team to Perry Barr and an immense assemblage of spectators gathered to witness the match. In 1881, you will remember, Queen's Park (commonly known as the 'Spiders') beat us by four goals to none and we thought it incumbent to put our strongest team in the field in order to get a chance of saving ourselves from another reverse. The game was splendidly contested from beginning to end; but we had reason to complain of a little hard luck, as twice a couple of well-aimed shots hit the posts and the ball rebounded into play. Our goalkeeper, on the other hand, saved innumerable shots and the Villa defence was, perhaps, one of the most striking features of the day's sport. You will guess from all this that I am about to prepare you for a tale of defeat, but it was only by one goal to nil, so that we were very far from coming out of the contest without honour.

"The back division of the Queen's Park showed marvellously good form, but it was not considered that their forwards were superior to ours. At half-time no goal had been scored on either side, though there had been some desperately hard work done. In the second part the visitors pressed us very hard and Vale was kept too busy to be quite comfortable. A bit of neat passing gave me a chance of scoring, but my final shot was magnificently punched out by McCullum. Then the visitors got the ball again and shot after shot was aimed at our goal, all without effect. Everybody was beginning to think that no score would be made on either side that afternoon, when a free kick near our fortress gave the visitors a much-desired chance and out of a scrimmage that followed, Christie, on the left, put the ball between the posts. And there the game ended."

"Did you play again the same week?"

"Yes, we played a friendly match on the following Saturday, although our exertions had thrown us a little off colour. The Wednesbury Old Athletics were our rivals and we beat them by three goals to none.

"The next week I captained the Birmingham team against Sheffield. This was an annual encounter which had taken place since 1877, with varying results. On one occasion we had been defeated by ten goals to nil, while at other times we had won comfortably. The previous year, however, as I have related in its place, we were beaten by five goals to two, so that the result of the contest was by no means safe to anticipate.

"We put a strong team in the field, but one of the selected players, Yates, the well-known Walsall half-back, had died early in the same week, his place being taken by Brandrick, of the same team. Mr. Yates was held in high esteem by us all and all the Birmingham players wore a crape mourning band round their left arm as a token of respect to his memory. This was Mr. Cofield's admirable idea.

"The match was in some respects a good one, though rather one-sided, as the Sheffielders played a very loose game at times, while the combination of the local forwards was generally admired. I had the good fortune to score the first point for our side, a quarter of an hour after the game commenced, from a corner kick splendidly placed by Brandrick. Before half-time Whateley had scored a second point for us after a brilliant run by Brodie and on a change of ends the Blades, roused by our success, commenced a vigorous attack in our territory.

We were, in consequence, obliged to play a strictly defensive game, but before very long the ball again got in our possession and Whateley gained a third goal and a fourth was not long in coming. It was a comfortable victory for us and highly popular.

"We next had the satisfaction," continued Archie, "of decisively beating the Walsall Swifts in the first round of the English Cup Competition. We won by five to one. It is a curious fact, perhaps worth mention, that I always was able to appear in my best form against the Walsall teams and on this occasion I had several runs which fairly set the spectators roaring. It was when playing against the Swifts once that my famous run took place and I passed four or five of my opponents, ending up with a goal."

"What was the next event of the season, Mr. Hunter?"

"The next event," replied Archie, "was what we call the Lancashire Trip. We travelled to Manchester and stayed at one of the hotels there, having plenty of fun in the evenings. We practically took possession of the smoke-room and with Mr. W. B. Mason (in command of the team) and his brother (our goalkeeper), Law and Apperley, we were kept in roars of laughter while a sing-song was improvised. I should like you to have seen Law, who was one of the most amusing and good-humoured fellows I ever met. Whenever you saw him he had a smile on his face and he laughed at his own jokes as loudly as anyone and everybody was sure to catch the infection and join him. He was in very good form all through the trip and with the other talent which the team possessed we had the merriest of times.

"From Manchester we went to Darwen and played them on the Saturday – a boisterous day. Ten minutes after the kick-off Eli Davis dribbled the leather along the left wing and made a fine shot into the mouth of the Darwen goal. J. Richmond met it with his hands, but the leather eluded him and dropped between the posts. This was good for us, but it was half an hour before we got another chance. Then a hot shot of mine went home. So far the wind had been in our favour and on changing ends the Darwen captain spurred on his men to take full advantage of the same circumstance. Hollis succeeded in scoring for his side soon after the resumption of play and a second point was added by Norris, but disputed. The referee decided in favour of Darwen and this made the score even. But scarcely a minute later a raid of ours on the Darwen goal led to a free kick being allowed and after a scrimmage Whateley put the ball through and scored the winning point. This was a sad shock to the Darwen spectators, who had enthusiastically cheered every success of the home team and had hoped we should be beaten.

"Another severe struggle was in store for us, however. We went to Alderley Edge on Sunday. On the Monday we met the Blackburn Rovers, who were so hard to beat on their own ground. In spite of the fact that a hailstorm was raging, two thousand spectators assembled to witness the contest. The play was brilliant on both sides and before half-time neither scored. Afterwards, Roberts secured his maiden point and it turned out that that was to be the only goal that day. We returned home flushed with victory."

"There was plenty to do when you got back, I suppose?"

"Yes. We had to play in several Cup ties and the following Saturday saw us engaged in battle at Halesowen, in connection with the Birmingham and District Association Cup. As we won by twelve goals to none I can leave you to judge of the nature of the game.

"Then came an encounter with Stafford Road in the second round of the Football Association Cup. This match, which we won by five goals to none, is chiefly memorable for the extraordinary spectacle we all presented when the game was over. A big fall of rain had made the ground sloppy and we soon found that we were playing in a thick mud pudding. Every run, every kick of the ball, caused ourselves and our comrades to be bespattered and when the game was over we looked like two-and-twenty barbarians with our native warpaint on. From head to foot we were simply plastered with mud and Apperley was so struck with the novelty of his appearance that he went straight away and sat for his portrait. If that portrait should ever be exhibited I wonder what people would think it represented?" – and as Archie said this he laughed heartily at the recollection. "On December 8th," Archie continued, "we met the Small Heath Alliance in a friendly match and won by four goals to none. As the weather was very favourable that afternoon there was a tremendous concourse of spectators who were quite satisfied with the day's sport. Arthur Brown, Whateley and myself had some excellent runs, but it was the following week which saw us really putting forth all we knew.

"This was when we met Cambridge University, a crack team, with such players as Spilsbury and Pawson in it, both grand dribblers and dead shots at goal. The match was played for the benefit of the Perry Barr Institute and although the day was far from pleasant 6,000 people assembled and there was a large muster of ladies. It will be best I think, if I describe this game in the words of others.

"This is what was written on the match at the time:- 'The company were compensated by one of the finest expositions of the dribbling game ever witnessed in the Midland counties. The game throughout was a magnificent one, both teams exhibiting splendid form. Every member of the University team played faultlessly. Their defence was unique, Mr. J. Rendall, their custodian, being many times applauded for the remarkable dexterity with which he averted some of the difficult shots from the Villa forwards. Davis was the only Villa representative who did not play up to his usual form, but in the second half of the game he showed greater dash and on several occasions placed the ball in dangerous proximity to the Cantabs' goal and it was from a splendid centre of his that Brown secured the third goal.

"'The University won the toss and elected to play down hill and with a strong wind in their favour. Archie Hunter kicked off and Cobbold and Broughton immediately ran the ball down into the Villa territory, where, after a little give-and-take play, Dunn thus early in the game scored the first goal for the Light Blues. From the kick-off the home forwards made a short incursion into the visitors' quarters, but Squire promptly returned the ball and a passing run by the University men endangered the Villa fortress again and a second point was added by

Dunn. Thus the Cantabs secured a couple of goals before the game was ten minutes old. Roused by this the Villa afterwards played a much better and faster game and Apperley and Dawson neutralised the attempts made by the visitors. Still continuing to press the Villa, the University gained a corner kick, which was nicely placed by Cobbold, but Davis got possession and executed a good run. Passing the ball to Vaughton when well in the opposing territory, he made matters look exceedingly dangerous for the visitors, but Squire and Walters averted the danger and enabled Wilson to trouble the home team. Simmonds with a splendid long kick returned the ball to Whateley, who endeavoured to assume the aggressive, but Amos quickly sent the ball to mid-field. A continued rush of the home forwards placed the University goal in jeopardy and the centre by Davis was promptly converted into a goal by Vaughton. Later on Vaughton essayed a run, but Amos dispossessed him of the leather and with the long kick sent the ball flying down the field. Riddell passed to Archie Hunter who, not to be denied, executed a splendid run and gained a corner kick, which came to nothing. A canter down the field by Spilsbury and Pawson placed the Villa citadel in imminent danger, Vale having to use his hands in the defence of his charge, whilst Riddell twice headed the ball away. A splendid exhibition of passing by the Villa forwards almost resulted in a goal, Davis just missing a centre of Hunter's and Squire and Moore cleared the attack. The visitors continued to have a slight advantage until half-time, but the Villa played a strong defence and prevented any further score.

"'On the resumption the Villa played with great dash and having the advantage of the slope continually forced their opponents to play on the defensive and Rendall was cheered for the magnificent manner in which he returned the ball into play from the many shots of the Villa forwards. The visitors, after this, made an attempt to break away, but were unable to get farther than midfield before Apperley took the ball from them and passing to Brown, that player finished a splendid run with a shot at the University fortress; but the Cantab's custodian was not to be caught napping, as he promptly punched the ball out and gave a corner.

Still pressing the Villa, the visitors gained a corner soon afterwards, but the Villa made desperate attempts to score, several shots actually hitting the goal posts and rebounding into play. Eventually, however, they were rewarded for their exertions by the Villa captain equalising the score with a splendid screw shot. Encouraged by this success, the home forwards, immediately upon the ball being restarted, dashed away at a terrific pace and a grand centre of Davis's was very smartly and cleverly converted into a third goal by Brown. Further vigorous attacks resulted in nothing and towards the close of the game the University once more held the upper hand, Cobbold, by a fine shot, again putting the score on a par. Thus one of the best games witnessed this season ended in a draw – three goals each.'

"It was decidedly the best and most exciting game we had played," added Archie, "and I am pleased to say that it added a good sum to the funds of the Institute for whose benefit we had played. Two more matches remained for the year – one against the Walsall Swifts which we unexpectedly lost by two goals to none, chiefly on account of having unreliable substitutes for four or five absentee members of the team. The second match was with the Wednesbury Old Athletics. Our opponents began by scoring three goals in succession; we replied with one; the Old Uns scored again; so did we, never giving them another chance and winning by seven to four.

"What was the net result of the 1883-4 season, Mr. Hunter?"

"Well, without now entering into details of other matches played during the season, I can give you an account of the final incidents in this part of our career. But in order to avoid telling too much of myself and so that all the points may be dealt with, the following summary and description might be well introduced. The Birmingham and District Association Challenge Cup was the great prize we aimed at keeping in our possession. In the Final Tie we had to meet the Walsall Swifts and no one thought we should have much difficulty in bringing off the event. This conclusion was justified and the following spirited narrative will give you the history of the Cup and how we won it.

'The old cup has done yeoman service for the pastime, indeed there can be no doubt that, but for the enormous amount of interest it infused into the game, we should not have made such rapid strides as we have done. The trophy under mention was first offered for competition in 1876 and it first found a resting place in Wednesbury, the Old Athletic Club defeating Stafford Road in the final by three goals to two. In the season of 1877-9 the Old Athletic fell a prey to the prowess of that then splendid organisation, the Shrewsbury Club and the final was that year fought out by the latter and the powerful Wednesbury Strollers team, the Salopians winning by two goals to one. It is a remarkable fact that two players on the side of the losers were last Saturday to be found in the ranks of the winners; I refer to Eli Davis and Alf Harvey, who were then the two finest left-wingers in the district. The Villa were not a very powerful lot at this time, the Saltley Collegians (then a remarkably good eleven) extinguishing their chances by the large score of four goals to nil.

'The next season once more found the indomitable Old Uns in the final and again success crowned their efforts, Stafford Road having to eat the leek for the second time. Very early in the next season the holders, the W.O.A.C. had to lay aside all claims to the Cup, the Small Heath Alliance, who fortunately for them, had to contest their match with them on the very day that Reeves, the crack Wednesbury left-wing forward, was united in the bonds of holy matrimony and so evil were the effects of the festivities indulged in on 'that auspicious occasion' by the Athletics, that the Heathens left the field with a goal to the good. The winners turned up in the person of the Villa, who easily beat an eleven representing Saltley College, in the deciding match.

'The next year saw a remarkable improvement in the play of the Birmingham cracks, who inflicted disastrous defeats on some of the finest organisations of the day. A defeat of six goals to nothing that they inflicted on the Old Athletics made the Cup look a certainty for them, but in the final the Swifts tore the laurels from the brow, defeating them, after a terrific struggle, by a solitary point to nothing. The losers were by far the better team, but a goal secured early in the afternoon gave the Swifts a chance. They all immediately fell back on their goal and refused to quit it; as a consequence even the brilliant forward play of the Villa was powerless against the efforts of half a score of backs and goalkeeper that has scarcely seen an equal.

'In the following year the Villa had their revenge, licking their former victors in the semi-final by exactly the same score that they themselves had been defeated and followed up this success by securing the verdict in the final struggle after a tough fight with the Old Athletics. Last season the same clubs met under the same conditions and once more victory rested with the Perry Barr representatives. The excitement caused by the meeting of the Swifts and the Villa in former years was modified to a great extent in 1884, this no doubt being caused by the immense supe-riority the Villa possesses over any other local combination. There were very few yells from brakes full of excited Black-countrymen, every bit of good play was cheered with pleasing impartiality, but the excitement was never up to fever heat.

'The game, in the first-half, was of a most exciting nature, the Swifts' forwards putting in a lot of good offensive work, whilst it goes without saying that their defence was of the highest order. The Villa team has for some little time been a trifle off-colour and Simmonds, Whateley, Archie Hunter and Roberts have not been in the best of health; indeed, the Villa skipper was suffering from a fearful bruise which many thought would materially affect his playing powers. As it happened, however, the locals turned out in capital fettle and although Archie was at an undoubted disadvantage, he so far succeeded in forgetting his sores as to be once more the best forward on the field. The game was very fiercely contested up to half-time and when the first forty-five minutes had elapsed the Walsall men were only one goal to the bad and that was a rather fluky one, the wind carrying a rather high shot by Archie Hunter through the posts, Sheldon being completely baffled by the sudden change of direction the ball assumed.

'Three minutes after the second half had been entered upon the Villa secured a second point, a beautiful fast shot from the foot of Howard Vaughton whizzing past Sheldon, who could only touch the sphere with the tip of his fingers. This second reverse so exasperated the Walsall captain that he ordered Sheldon out of goal and took the position himself. In the meantime, the Swifts' forwards went to work in fine style and repeatedly pressed the Villa backs, but were invariably repulsed. The Villa thus won by four goals to none – a fifth was put on one second after the whistle had blown, but of course, that was not allowed. The Villa put in some of the prettiest passing I have seen them indulge in for some time and several times they came from the centre of the field right to the Swifts' goal, their clever interchanges completely puzzling the Swifts' backs and against a team with less powerful defence they would have dotted up a large score.

'Vaughton and Archie fairly carried off the forward honours, the former giving one of the most polished and finished expositions of the game it has ever been my lot to witness. Morris could never touch him and the clever little international man eluding him with the utmost ease on nearly every occasion they met. Once he came fully three parts of the length of the field and dodging Morris almost on the goal-line, centred clean across the mouth of the Swifts' goal, Arthur Brown just missing a glorious chance. Archie Hunter astonished the folks by the nimble manner in which he skipped about the field and with the dexterity with which he avoided his opponents. His dribbling was characterised with all its old neatness and he shot at goal with great precision and vigour. Whateley made very few mistakes and his exhibition had many good points. Brown, who is in great form just now, played quite his old game and delighted the spectators with his clever dodges.

'The left wing did not put in the amount of work they generally do, but very little fault could be found with the little they did do. Freddy Dawson was the hero of the first part of the game, but he fell off a little towards the close. Time after time he fairly brought down the house by his dashing play and during the initial portion Horton and Mills scarcely ever got away. His heading was very clever, his tackling superb and the dash that he infused into his play quite won the hearts of all sections of the public. Apperley worked all through in his consistently good style, as the brilliancy of his heading was ever apparent. He scarcely appeared to such advantage as Dawson, but this is fully accounted for by the fact that Davis and Farmer, the pair to whom he was opposed, were far in advance of Horton and Mills, who were looked after by Dawson. They understood each other's movements well and passed from one to the other very accurately, thus placing Apperley at a distinct disadvantage. Simmonds and Riddell did all that they were asked to in rare style, Joey's tackling and Riddell's heading being particularly admired. Harvey had not much to do, but made one or two smart things.

'The Swifts played a good sound game, one that a year or two ago would have caused them to be looked upon as prodigies. Their forwards were a trifle disorganised at times, it is true, but then the excellence of their rivals made this more apparent than it really was. Higgins was by far the best of the forwards, his neat style of dribbling and passing making him a great favourite with the spectators. Farmer and Davies each did excellent work and gave the Villa defenders some hard work. Neither Mills nor Horton did anything worth recording and both were completely sat upon by Dawson whenever they made any attempt to get away.

'The half-back play of the Swifts was excellent, Allen being by far the best of a capital triplet. He stuck to Archie like a shadow and was not altogether unsuccessful in his tussles with the Villa skipper. Brandrick did more than one clever thing. Morris did not play so strong a game as usual, Howard Vaughton fairly making circles round him, whilst Whateley always sailed past him with the greatest ease. Jones was a tower of strength to his team and in the first half his heading and heavy kicking frequently saved his side from disaster. I don't think he has improved much of late, but he is still a rare back. Aldridge must also come in for favourable criticism, as he never made the shadow of a mis-kick throughout the whole ninety minutes' play. Sheldon, whilst he was in goal, repulsed many hot shots in his best style and not the slightest blame can be attached to him for the two points that were scored against him.

'In conclusion, I must not forget to heartily congratulate the Villa Club upon attaining the proud position of 'possessors' of the Birmingham Cup, as this being the third consecutive occasion on which they have won the trophy, it now remains in their possession permanently. This is the first time that it has been won outright and it is a gratifying fact that the club that has done more than any other to raise the tone of Midland football should be the lucky recipients of the cup.'

"With this high tribute," added Archie, "we were content and after so hard a season the leather-chasers entered upon a well-earned rest until the dark days began to come round again."

Chapter 13

The Villa and 'The Spiders'

"I come now," said Archie Hunter as he settled himself down for a chat and looked as if he had something particularly pleasant to tell, "I come now to the time when we had a series of contests with big clubs. It was our ambition to defeat, some time or other, such strong teams as the Blackburn Rovers, the Bolton Wanderers and Queen's Park.

"Whenever we met these teams we fought our best and ofttimes made a very close thing of the result. But it was a long time before anything very decisive happened on our side, though occasionally we ourselves experienced a reverse that you might have thought would dishearten us. I gave you last week an instance of how Queen's Park beat us on our ground in the October of 1883 and that was the third time our friends had assembled at Perry Barr only to find it once more proved that the Villa were not yet up to the form of the famous Scotch club. 'The Spiders,' in fact, seemed to be invincible so far as we were concerned, though we were always glad to play them for two reasons – first, they played a grand game and secondly, they were an excellent set of fellows. After the match it was our custom to meet socially at a dinner given to the visiting team and we drank healths and made complimentary speeches until the hour of parting.

"Well, with a defeat of four to one against us and specially anxious to convert this into victory on the very first opportunity, we travelled to Glasgow in 1884, again to test our powers. In the first week of the new year, I may incidentally mention, we had met the Staveley club, in connection with the Birmingham Association Cup and after a rough game defeated them by three goals to none. Since then we had gone in for strict training and we began to think that we might prove equal to the occasion. Of course, we had plenty of fun on the journey up. We started on the Friday morning, all in good trim and the comic element was not lacking. Two of the team – I won't mention their names – in order to show their enthusiasm on visiting Scotland and to mark their sympathy with the customs of the country, treated us to a little exhibition which provoked the greatest amusement. One of them wrapped a great plaid shawl round him and by a little dexterous arrangement of his ordinary clothing, stood forth in all his glory as a Highland chief. The other had equipped himself with some miniature bagpipes, which he played with frantic energy in the most discordant style. At every station one would pop his head out of the carriage window and ask –

'How long do we stay here, porter?'

'Two minutes, sir,' would be the reply.

"Out would jump our two merry friends immediately and take their places on the platform. The piper struck up the music, which might be supposed to be a Scotch air by people of strong imagination and the Highland chief would execute the fling, to the amazement of all the good folks in the vicinity. This little comedy created as much sensation at some places as if the Highland chief had come with his clan to avenge the massacre of Glencoe. We dined at Carlisle, enjoyed a ramble and then went on to Glasgow, arriving late in the evening. But there were restless spirits with us still who could not prepare quietly for the next day's work.

"I knew that early in the morning a number of excursion trains would arrive bringing large numbers of spectators from the towns in the district. About four o'clock I was awakened by a great tramping of feet and the shouts of excited voices. 'Good gracious' I thought to myself, 'these trippers are coming in early and making a great row,' But what surprised me most of all was that the noise seemed to come from the corridors of the hotel, which were about fifty yards long and a good width. Presently I jumped out of bed, determined to see what was the matter. And what do you think it was? The more ardent supporters of our team, instead of resting quietly in bed and letting others rest also, were handicapping one another and racing in the corridors. They kept the sport up until breakfast-time and there was no more sleep for any of us, however tired we might be. The day turned out badly. When we reached the ground, where an immense throng had gathered, the rain was pouring down in torrents and looked as if it would last for hours. But this seemed to make no difference to the visitors, who watched the game from beginning to end with unabating interest. We played at Titwood Park and the ground was in a sodden state. There was a sort of superstition on the part of many footballers in regard to this game. They believed that the fourth round of the competition for the National Challenge Cup always brought bad luck to the Villa."

"What was the reason of this, Mr. Hunter?"

"In the first place," Archie replied, "people remembered the result of the match against Notts County in the fourth round for the Cup the previous season and it was a disappointment to our own supporters that we had been obliged to play each round on our opponents' ground. Feeling against the Association in regard to this particular draw had run rather high for a time, but our committee had been among the first to record their confidence in those who had the management of these affairs. But another difficulty had arisen, which at one time seemed likely to stop the match. Queen's Park were engaged to play their Scotch Tie with the Hibernians at Edinburgh on January 19th, having only January 12th open. But we had just been playing a couple of tough matches in which several of our team had been injured and we declined to meet Queen's Park until these men had a chance of recovering. Queen's Park, therefore, obtained leave from the Scottish Association to extend the time for playing off the Scotch Tie and this was particularly gratifying to us all.

"So great was the interest in the match that special trains were run from Birmingham to Glasgow and thousands of lovers of the game travelled up by them. Besides that, four thousand people had assembled on the platform to see us off and to give us a hearty cheer and an equally hearty welcome was accorded to us when we arrived in Glasgow. It was all this which made us so desirous of acquitting ourselves well and when we went on the field, every man being determined to do his best, we had hopes of victory. Ringing cheers greeted both the teams when they appeared and then the huge concourse settled down to watch the sport. We won the toss and I elected to defend top goal, having a slight incline in our favour.

"At five minutes to three Dr. Smith commenced hostilities and our work began. The doctor's fine dribbling powers were soon displayed and he and Harrower by a well-executed run brought the ball dangerously near our goal. Apperley and Dawson frustrated the attempt to score and Christie was the next man to get a chance and he dashed off at a tremendous pace, forcing us to play on the defensive. I had the good fortune to get on the ball soon after and had a run up the field and eluded the Queen's Park forwards, but the back division was too strong for me. The people cheered the effort, however and after some give and take play Queen's Park gained a corner and Fraser placed the ball neatly in front of our goal. Eli Davis cleared and after a corner had fallen to us and resulted in nothing, Campbell got the ball at his toe and with a quick long shot scored the first point for Queen's Park within ten minutes of the commencement of the game. On resuming, Dr. Smith was conspicuous for another brilliant run and our goalkeeper was kept on the alert watching a vigorous scramble. Presently he sent out two most dangerous shots, but we had the greatest difficulty in preventing a score. The play was extremely hot and fast for a time, but getting on the ball at last I commenced, with Arthur Brown, to attack our opponents' fortress. The ball passed from one to the other, but was at length unfortunately shot out close by the home team's timbers. Hard pressed, or pressing hard in turn, we managed to maintain our ground and at last Whateley made off with the ball, finishing with a long shot at the Queen's Park citadel and although the ball went wide the 'Daisy-cutter' was loudly applauded for this plucky effort to lower the opposing colours.

"By half-time the home team had scored again and our own record was blank. After the rest a very easy goal was obtained within a minute or two by Christie who, during the whole of the day was in excellent form and contributed greatly to the success of his team. Another point was added by Dr. Smith and though we made things look none too pleasant for our rivals their defence was too good and we could accomplish nothing. The fifth goal aroused the wildest enthusiasm and when Dr. Smith, just as the game was concluding, scored again the tumultuous applause was overwhelming. Yet the game was not yet over. Whateley got the ball at his toe and a few moments before time shot it through the posts. At this a cheer went up from the supporters of both teams, for this was the first goal the Villa had ever scored against Queen's Park. Our defeat by six goals to one did not dishearten us so much as it would have done, when we reflected that at last we had broken through the Queen's Park defence. That was almost a victory for us.

"We were handicapped slightly by the indisposition of Whateley and Roberts and the state of the ground seriously impeded us, Vaughton, for example, missed a beautiful chance of scoring, his toe sticking in the mud and only just lifting the ball where the opposing goalkeeper could easily get at it. In fact, two clear goals were lost at the very commencement of the game, but I am very doubtful as to whether we could possibly have won that day. Anderson and Fraser, for Queen's Park, forwards on the right, were in splendid form and Apperley could do nothing with them. Our backs, Simmonds and Riddell, were very useful and Simmonds was at times brilliant. Christie, the Queen's Park forward on the left, played a dashing game, though some of us thought that he was occasionally 'off-side.' Walter Arnott was too much for Eli Davis and Charlie Campbell, who captained the opposing team was never seen to better advantage. Arthur Brown and I did our best, but had difficulty in coping with the rival backs. The opinion after the match was that nothing could beat Queen's Park and we returned home with one more defeat at their hands to add to our list."

"When did you next meet Queen's Park, Mr. Hunter?"

"Not until the following November," Archie replied, "when they came down to play us on our own ground at Perry Barr. It was a memorable day. Remember that time after time we had made scarcely any headway against them and that in spite of the number of matches we had played we had scored only one goal against them. Then remember that this club had carried off the Scottish Cup seven times out of a possible ten and that they had only been defeated in the final for the English Cup by the Blackburn Rovers by two goals to one. And now here was this great combination once more opposed to us! The idea of defeating the 'Spiders' was almost too much to imagine. Our team had somewhat changed during the season and among the newcomers were Price and Riddell. The latter, who was very tall, earned the curious nickname of 'The Telescopic Neck' owing to a way which he had of shooting his head out towards the ball when the goal was in danger. His neck was long and his head could be seen above all others working in a surprising way. Price was a persevering player, but otherwise was not remarkable. Harvey was now our goal in the place of Vale, but the others were in their usual places, the team being composed as follows:- Harvey, goal; Riddell and Simmonds, backs; F. Dawson and G. Price, half-backs; Whateley and Albert Brown, right wing; Archie Hunter and Arthur Brown, centres; Vaughton and Davis, left wing. I do not think that the Scotchmen sent us down their best representatives, for there were several notable absentees – Arnott, Fraser, Kerr and Campbell among the number. Still they were a grand lot and the team was as follows:- McCullum, goal; McDougall and Harvie, backs; Macare and McDonald, half-backs; W. Anderson and McWhennell, right wing; Harrower and Miller, centres; Christie and Allan, left wing. They arrived in Birmingham in the small hours of Saturday morning, rather fatigued with their journey.

"The contest excited more interest than any other match I remember up to that time. The gate was enormous, over twelve thousand people being on the ground. In the town the excitement was at fever-heat. Buses, brakes, cabs and cars had been carrying down the crowd all the morning and the railway company's special trains were insufficient for the multitude requiring conveyance. Troops of men could be seen in the roads leading to the Villa ground and the one topic of conversation in the town seemed to be the chance we had of beating the yet unbeaten team from over the border. Queen's Park were always favourites with the Birmingham public and as they bowled along in their brake to the field they were cordially cheered by the crowd. Another cheer greeted them as Anderson, with his hands thrust in his pockets, led them from the pavilion. The Villa, naturally, received plenty of encouragement and no sooner had we begun to take up our positions than pigeons could be seen flying from all parts bearing away the news that the battle had begun.

"We lost the toss and had to play uphill with a stiff wind against us. I kicked off and we invaded the Queen's Park territory. A corner kick fell to the visitors, but Riddell cleared; a long kick by Miller, however, kept the ball hovering in our quarters. Some fine passing by Whateley and the two Browns made affairs look perilous for the Scotchmen, but McDougall got the ball back and a shot from another player sent the ball into Harvey's hands. He returned the ball into play and Albert Brown went away with a rush, but Harvey in brilliant style tackled him and the ball went out. Simmonds next had some hard work to do and saved some hard shots. Two corners fell to the visitors and the second one made the prospect look dark for us; but Harvey was equal to the occasion and punched the leather out of goal admirably. Whateley took the ball up field and passed to me, but McDougall was waiting and we were again repulsed. A few minutes later a splendid exhibition of passing by Albert Brown, Vaughton and Whateley carried the ball into the enemy's quarters and roused intense enthusiasm. The younger Brown then sent the ball flying into McCullum's hands, but the latter saved his goal and some scientific play which followed drew forth the acclamations of the crowd. Christie next put us on our defence and after some hot shots the visitors gained another corner kick. This was placed right in the mouth of our goal, but Freddy Dawson came to the rescue and the now baffled 'Spiders' came down on us with renewed vigour and attempted to score. A scrimmage ensued and out of this Anderson put the leather through, scoring the first goal, five minutes before half-time.

" The spectators greeted the success of the visitors with a loud round of applause as the excitement now reached fever heat. No further score was effected when ends were changed and having the wind in our favour we now played a more aggressive game than before. We were urged on by the shouts of our supporters, who expected us to make a bold bid for success. Davis and Vaughton took the ball down the field and a long and continuous attack on the Queen's Park timbers resulted. Obtaining possession on the right wing I put the ball into McCullum's hands and from his return the ball struck Arthur Brown's knee and rebounded through goal, the score thus being equalised.

"The applause was uproarious and hats and sticks were thrown into the air by the enthusiastic crowd. Our hearts beat wildly when the ball was started again. Christie put in a magnificent run and centred which evoked cheers, but Riddell repulsed him. Nevertheless we were severely pressed, for the Queen's Park men were making strenuous exertions to score the winning point. Harvey was kept busy and did his work manfully and the critical nature of the game affected the onlookers considerably. Putting on an extra spurt we took the ball into the opposition territory and were several times within an ace of scoring. Darkness, however, was coming on rapidly and each side played a desperate game. Misjudged kicks were not uncommon, for it was hard to keep cool. At last we secured a corner, the first we had had that day and though it was unproductive, we kept the ball in the opposition territory. A final shot of mine caused the ball to strike the post and it rebounded into play. Vaughton kicked over in self-defence; Eli Davis took the corner grandly and a rush on our part resulted in the ball going through off Albert Brown. This was the winning point.

"Only a few minutes remained and then Major Marindin sounded the whistle and the Villa had won at last – won by two goals to one. I cannot attempt to describe the scene that followed, the vociferous cheers that greeted us cannot be described in words. The people rushed over the field shouting as long as they had voices left; they shook us by the hand until our joints were in danger; they patted us on the backs until we were sore. I doubt whether many people went home that day with the same hats they brought out and lost property in the shape of walking-sticks and umbrellas would have made a good stock for a second-hand dealer. At night people went about singing a ballad, with a refrain, 'The Villa have licked Queen's Park' and I was followed home by a multitude roaring as if I had won the battle of Waterloo."

"I suppose you have had some curious experiences in this respect?"

"Yes. There was one old gentleman who was in the habit of rushing forward at the end of a game and holding my hand in a tight grip until I had walked off the field. Nothing could induce him to loose it. Then there were those who thought that the highest compliment they could pay us was to deliver thumps upon the back and their aim was not always true, but fell upon the neck or head, or anywhere. I have been carried shoulder-high, too, but how that came about belongs to another occasion."

"To what do you attribute your final success over Queen's Park?" I asked.

"To our superior combination," Archie replied. "Everyone congratulated us for the way in which we played together. Our combination was the theme of admiration."

"And the Villa combination, I have heard, was mainly due to your exertions," I said.

"That is what people say," said Archie "and you must remember that I had a very good set of players to deal with too. As for Queen's Park, they took their reverse well and like the good fellows they were, complimented us upon at last turning the tables upon them. The Birmingham public has always looked forward to later visits of the Queen's Park and is surprised and disappointed that of late the committee has not been able to arrange for another match.

"After this splendid victory over Queen's Park, however, we experienced a defeat from the Bolton Wanderers, but to give you a good account of our contests with the famous club and with several others the same season, I shall require another chapter. I may mention, however, that in the first part of 1884-5 season we were defeated by the Sheffield Wednesday by three goals to two: The Villa played some new men on the occasion and as I was not present myself I cannot give you any details of the game. It was an unlucky start for us, however, this being our opening match. Late in October we drew with Derby Midland, but I and four others of the team were playing for Birmingham against Sheffield that day. Wednesbury Town suffered a defeat at our hands in November in the first round for the Football Association Challenge Cup, the scores being Villa 4 and Wednesbury Town 1. The latter part of the game was played in a thick mist and the players could hardly distinguish one another. Wednesbury Town was then a new club which was intended to succeed the Old Athletic. It promised very well and had one or two good seasons; but I heard no more of it after a time. We scored two goals against Walsall Town in December in connection with the same competition and meeting Wednesbury Town again a fortnight later we defeated them by four to one. In the meantime, we had played Cambridge University and this time won by three to one.

"The 1884-5 season was noted rather for close matches than for a series of victories scored off teams of only second-rate importance and the record for the six months was:- Matches played, 47; won, 24; lost, 14; drawn, 9; goals gained, 114; goals lost, 86. These figures do not look quite so well as some I have already given you, but you will see by further details that our work was quite as good, if not better, than that we had done before."

Chapter 14

The Chief Incidents in the 1884-5 Season

"I promised earlier," said Archie Hunter, "to give you an account of the remaining incidents of importance in our 1884-5 season, which included the encounters with Queen's Park which I have already described.

"The season had its notable reverses as well as its triumphs and you will be occasionally astonished to hear of a big victory one week being followed a week later by a defeat for the Villa at the hands of what we should consider an inferior combination. All sorts of minor circumstances might be taken into consideration to account for eccentric cases like these, but I suppose that after all we made a special effort when we knew that it was necessary and at other times, knowing our reputation was not at stake, we took matters easily, often too easily, as the sequel shows.

"On October 4th 1884, we met the Bolton Wanderers, who came down to Perry Barr. Both sides put their strongest team into the field, Struthers being the only notable absentee of the Wanderers and Appleby being the only missing Villan. The Villa and the Wanderers at this time were about equally matched and a close finish was expected. Nor were the spectators disappointed. The Wanderers started the ball up the hill and at once began to press us hard, while a number of miskicks by the Villa forwards gave them the opportunity of continuing the aggressive. After one or two dangerous shots had been averted, however, we got the ball well down the field and Whateley finished by sending in a splendid shot, which was cleverly saved by Bateson, the goalkeeper. After this the visitors had the best of the play again and Hewitson, getting possession of the ball, broke away and secured a goal almost before we perfectly realised that our citadel was in danger. It was particularly smart work and had the effect of rousing us.

"The defence of the Wanderers, however, was so good that all our efforts to score were without effect. A long kick of Dawson, one of our half-backs, sent the ball to mid-field, from where Hewitson attempted another run, but he was frustrated this time by Simmonds, who received much applause for the gallant and successful manner in which he tackled him. The first half of the game, in fact, was most hotly contested, but when the whistle sounded we had to play uphill, with the score still standing at one to none against us. After a short interval I restarted the leather and we commenced to play up vigorously.

"Three times Albert Brown made a splendid attempt to score and twice he was doomed to disappointment; but the third time he was avenged for his bad luck, for the ball went through, Bateson almost falling full length in his effort to stop it. The equalising of the score was loudly cheered by the spectators and encouraged by our success we kept the citadel of the Wanderers in an almost continual state of siege. I am credited with having made a good run just at this juncture. A critical spectator wrote:- 'Archie Hunter now got possession of the ball and put in the grandest run of the afternoon. Man after man was left behind by the Villa skipper, who eventually burst clean through the backs and sent in a lightning-paced shot which Bateson's body very luckily saved.' Bateson had to give a corner in self-defence, but no material advantage resulted, though the visitors appeared to be having the worst of the struggle.

"'Time' was now drawing near and it looked as if the game would result in a draw, though each side was making a desperate struggle to add another point to its score. The spectators showed signs of intense excitement and every advantage on either side drew from them shouts and comments and cheers. Riddell's 'telescopic neck' came in useful in stopping an almost certain shot of Steel's and then a rush of the Wanderers resulted in the ball going through, only to be instantly ruled off-side, however, as we had appealed just before the point was made. We were now at fever-heat, for every moment we expected the end to come. In the midst of this hot struggle the Bolton men broke away and a long shot from mid-field by Kennedy sent the leather into the mouth of goal and Davenport charging Harvey, the ball went through, the visitors thus scoring the winning point within a few seconds of time."

"You considered that rather hard lines, I suppose?"

"Well, when both sides are so anxious to score such things happen, although it is, of course, disappointing to the losing team to see the ball go through at the last moment. We felt our reverse rather keenly, but the game was a beautiful one from start to finish from a scientific point of view.

"We hoped to turn the tables on our Bolton friends when we met them in the following November, but the task was rendered the more difficult by the state of the ground, which was like a quagmire. This was our fourth meeting with the Wanderers, only one of which had resulted so far in a victory for the Villa. We went to Manchester on the Friday and arrived at Bolton the following morning.

"Between seven and eight thousand spectators had assembled to witness the contest, in which immense interest was taken. Struthers scored the first goal and Arthur Brown equalised matters soon afterwards. Play on both sides was of the most spirited character and when half-time was called we were two goals to the bad. The Villa forwards commenced working their hardest, but it was too late and at the call of time the Wanderers were proclaimed victors by four goals to one. The victory was naturally a source of great local enthusiasm; but although we regretted our defeat we could afford still to be satisfied with ourselves, for earlier in the same month we had defeated the English Cup holders, the Blackburn Rovers. This was a memorable achievement and makes November 1st 1884, a red-letter day in our calendar. The visit of this redoubtable team had been looked forward to with the highest interest and the splendid manner in which the Rovers had come out of the Cup competition the previous year had made every lover of the game expect a grand exposition of the game by them. We had not very great hopes of being able to beat the Cup holders and we were mostly anxious to avoid a severe drubbing.

"Early in the day all the roads leading to our ground presented an animated appearance, pedestrians on the way down and scores of cabs, cars and brakes forming a continuous stream to the gates at Perry Barr.

"It was not long after the game had begun that we began to put forth our strength and I participated in a neat run, in which Davis and Whateley took part and a score appeared imminent. McIntyre, who played an excellent game all day, cleared the attack and the game became terribly fast, the Rovers, I think, having slightly the worst of it on the whole. The ball was once put through our posts, but the referee promptly disallowed the point on account of off-side. A combined run by the whole string of the Blackburn forwards now made affairs look gloomy for us, but Simmonds, whose play was characterised by plenty of dash, came to the assistance of Riddell in repulsing the onslaught.

"Getting the ball into our possession again we commenced raining in shots in furious style, but they were skilfully saved by the Rovers' goalkeeper, Arthur. The leather now began to fly about the field with marvellous rapidity and after Arthur had punted out a long-dropping shot by Price, Albert Brown got the ball through and registered the first point for the Villa. Only two minutes later we were again round the visitors' stronghold and a centre by Albert Brown was cleverly converted into a goal by Howard Vaughton. This rapid scoring on our part evoked much acclamation from the multitude of onlookers, who indulged in the usual demonstrations and again showed their perfect willingness to run the risk of losing hats and sticks and handkerchiefs in order to testify their joy of a Villa victory.

"At half-time the Rovers had still failed to score, but we expected to find it harder to hold our own afterwards, as our opponents would have the wind and hill in their favour. Immediately on resuming they strove to make the best of these advantages and assumed the offensive. Our goalkeeper was equal to the emergency, however and defended his charge in masterly style, although, as someone said, it 'seemed a million to one against his saving' on one occasion.

"Some fine dribbling was seen in the course of the further proceedings and James Brown, one of the Blackburn centres, took the ball the length of the field and was only stopped by Simmonds when near our goal. Albert Brown then raced off swiftly up the right and there was seen a magnificent display of goalkeeping such as I have rarely witnessed. Albert Brown, Whateley and I put in some hot shots, which Arthur repulsed in a simply miraculous manner.

"Ten minutes before the close of the game a miskick by Riddell gave the visitors an opportunity of scoring and Harper, with a cross shot, scored the first and only goal for the Rovers. Thus winning by two to one we were entitled to feel some amount of satisfaction with ourselves considering the strength and the reputation of the team we had beaten.

"On leaving the field a huge friendly reception awaited us and we departed with the cheers of the great concourse still ringing in our ears. This triumph had followed fast upon another which was very noteworthy in its way.

"On October 20th we had met the Blackburn Olympic and opinion had been greatly divided as to the result of the contest. Up to that time our team had been off colour and on one or two occasions made a very poor exhibition on the field, while the Olympic had begun the season remarkably well. Although the wishes of our own friends were with us I doubt whether any of them would have felt inclined to take odds against the Olympic.

"As it happened, however, we played in our old form that day and though pressed hard by expert players we won by four goals to none. The first goal was scored by me, the second by Arthur Brown and the third by Whateley; the fourth was gained just at the last moment and put the finishing touch to a game which had been in our favour from beginning to end.

"But the last match of the year was to witness our utter discomfiture at the hands of the same team and once more we had an evidence of how thoroughly luck may change in football affairs. We journeyed to Blackburn to play the match and a hard prolonged frost had made the ground slippery, while its uneven nature in parts caused us to feel as if we were running on broken bricks. We had to be very careful indeed how we played, lest by a fall we should injure ourselves upon the hard iron-like ground. As you know the Villa were a fair-weather team and were seldom seen to advantage when the elements were unfavourable. The Olympians, on the other hand, surprised us by seeming to be pretty much at their ease upon the slippery surface. It was observed that we were slow in our passing and erratic in our shooting and without wishing to underrate the victory achieved by the other side, I think I may say that the state of the ground acted as an impediment to our success.

"After about a quarter of an hour's play Dewhurst, on the Olympic right, made a capital shot and alighted near the posts, where it bounded in the air and went over Harvey's head through the goal. At half-time we were three goals behind and we felt that the Olympic were turning the tables on us with a vengeance. We had seldom had a chance of scoring and the attempts we made had failed owing to the good defence of our opponents. We hovered about the Olympians' goal at times, but more frequently they were in our territory giving us plenty of work to do and finally they defeated us by five goals to one.

"In the new year, 1885, we met West Bromwich Albion in the third round of the National Association Challenge Cup, but no goals were scored and an exciting match was declared drawn. In consequence of this we met the team again the following Saturday in dreadfully bad weather, the rain falling in torrents the whole of the afternoon and the wind blowing a hurricane. The ground was consequently in as bad a state as it could be and the players were liberally bespattered, especially during the scrimmages.

"Once more I have a tale of defeat to tell and we were not unprepared for this, as the Albion had been playing up remarkably well and although the elements were so unfavourable they exhibited good style on this critical occasion. Some of the Villans were far from being in their usual form and taken altogether we played without much spirit.

"Of course there was plenty of good work done, but the Albion had much their own way and at half-time had scored twice, while we had failed to get the ball through their posts. Just as the second part of the game commenced the storm increased and half the time the players were rolling about the sodden field and covering themselves with more mud than glory. Towards the end of the game we made several desperate attempts to turn the tide, but we were baffled and the game ended in a victory for the Albion by three goals to none.

"The team to whom this victory fell was a right worthy one and I will give you their names:- Roberts, goal; H. Green and H. Bell, backs; E. Horton, Bunn and Stanton, half-backs; Woodall, Aston, Bayliss, Gooch and G. Bell, forwards.

"The following week, I am sorry to say, the popular Howard Vaughton received a severe injury while we were playing the Derby Midlands and had to be carried off the field."

"Your were still engaged in other Cup competitions, I believe, Mr. Hunter?"

"Oh, yes. We had yet to play off several rounds in the competition for the Birmingham Association Challenge Cup. On January 24th we drew with Staveley, each side scoring a goal and several friendly matches followed, notably one with the Great Lever team, whom we met for the first time in February and defeated by three goals to one.

"Accrington, who had come to the front, were also our rivals in the course of the same month and we enjoyed a very closely-contested game with them. In the first half our opponents, assisted by a high wind, had matters much their own way and scored three times; in the second half, when we had the same advantage, we scored three times also. Just as the whistle was about to blow Accrington scored again and consequently a rather curious day's sport ended in their favour.

"The following week, while we were playing a rather poor team sent down by Oxford University, whom we defeated by three goals to one, the final tie in the English Association Cup was being played by Queen's Park and Notts County and of course, attracted the attention of all lovers of the game. Ten to fifteen thousand people witnessed that game, which resulted in the victory of Queen's Park by two goals to one.

It is interesting to those who have taken an interest in the Villa to find that the team we had defeated in the November of 1884 afterwards achieved champion honours.

"I took part in a match between a representative eleven of Birmingham and District and an eleven selected from the Oxford and Cambridge teams in March, which resulted in a victory for us by three goals to one.

"Next we enjoyed another keen game with the West Bromwich Albion, who again proved to be our masters and defeated us by two to one. But you are, no doubt, waiting to hear how we fared in the competition which I mentioned just now. Well, it is a short story. Late in March we met the Wednesbury Old Athletics and after the game, which had no features of more than ordinary interest, ended in a win for by five goals to none.

"We had now to nerve ourselves to meet the Walsall Swifts in the final tie. The match was played on March 28th and this was the first competition for the new cup, the Villa, you will recollect, having secured absolute possession of the original cup by winning it three successive years.

"Five years before the Swifts had beaten us in the final round and speculation ran high as to whether they would this year repeat the performance. There was a tremendous muster of spectators and as the match was played at Aston most of these were our supporters and they did not forget to offer us the encouragement of their cheers whenever it was needed.

"At half-time the score stood:- Villa, 1; Swifts, 0 and at the end of the game we had only been able to get the leather through once more. But we had Been successful in our defence and thus the important match ended in a victory for the Villa by two to none and we gained possession of the new cup for the first year.

"The season was now nearly over. We defeated the celebrated Scotch organisation, Battlefield, by two goals to nil and the Corinthians, who included P. M. Walters, A. M. Walters, Spilsbury and Pawson in their team, by one to nil. The Corinthians had had a most successful tour and had defeated Preston North End by one goal to none, drawn with Derby County and then defeated them by two goals to one and beaten Blackpool by two goals to one. These were brilliant achievements and as the Corinthians up to this time had an unbeaten record there were many who thought they would prove too strong for the Villa. The two Walters played a grand game and Buckley and Ward, half-backs, were in excellent form. Our goal was secured right at the end of the game and thus we were the first to defeat this famous organisation.

"Next I must tell you how we met West Bromwich Albion again in the competition for the Mayor of Birmingham's Charity Cup and then proceed with details of our eventful 1885-6 season."

Chapter 15

A Long Season Ended and
a New One Begun

"This was the time," said Archie Hunter, as he took up the thread of his story of the 1884-5 season, "that the football season began when it liked and ended when it could. We did not, as a rule, begin playing much before September, but we never knew how long we might have to keep on. I have known clubs to play in June, when to say the least, the sport becomes a trifle too warm to be pleasant.

"In 1885 we played our last important match on May 26th and as that ended in a draw in connection with a Cup Tie, we ought still to have gone on playing; but for reasons which I shall presently state we were mercifully relieved and had a chance of taking a rest for three months. Last week I mentioned the match we played against the Corinthians, a picked team of London players chiefly assisted by some crack provincials.

"The two Walters were perhaps, even at that time, the most noted members and their reputations have grown considerably since that time. The brothers were both splendid players and when acting in unity, which was often the case, were in my opinion, the two finest backs in England. I had met them occasionally when playing against the Universities and when playing for Birmingham against the London Association. They were famous for their long kicks and the saying used to go that they could kick from one goal to the other. They showed excellent judgement also in tackling forwards when nearing goal and altogether were as strong and efficient a couple of players as you might meet with anywhere.

"I was also speaking to you last week of a series of contests the Villa waged with the West Bromwich Albion in which we got much the worst of it. In the middle of April, however, a change came o'er the spirit of their dream. We were drawn against the Albion in the tie for the Mayor of Birmingham's Charity Cup and great local interest centred in the match.

"The match was played at the Oval, Wood Green, Wednesbury and it is said that more than 12,000 spectators were present. All the week the Villa team had gone into strict training, for we felt that the encounter would have to be decisive.

"The game began evenly, but unfortunately, before many minutes had passed Horton, the captain of the Albion, was hurt and play had to be stopped for a time. On resuming, the Albion began to attack and a free kick to the West Bromwich then nearly proved disastrous. A good run by Eli Davis, Vaughton and myself then won a round of applause from the crowd and I finished with a shot into the opposing citadel which Roberts, the Albion goalkeeper, cleverly saved. The Albion then retaliated, but no score was gained.

"Albert Brown next dashed off with the ball and passing it smartly to me gave me a chance of putting it through the posts, the registration of the first point for the Villa calling forth cheers from our supporters. The Albion now began to press us hard and in turn were encouraged by the plaudits of their followers. Vaughton, however, raised the siege and before half-time was called Whateley scored a second point for us. This thoroughly roused our opponents, who began to play a desperately hard game, but we still had several attempts at scoring and Roberts was deservedly applauded for the skilful and dexterous manner in which he repelled our charges.

"Then came a lively incident. I sent the ball into the hands of Roberts and while he was in the act of stooping to pick it up Albert Brown rushed forward and sent him and the leather through the timbers. Poor Roberts received a kick which rendered him *hors de combat* for a time, though the occurrence was purely accidental.

"With a score of three against our opponents' none we resumed play with a good heart, but the tide turned and Bayliss, one of the forwards, scored for the Albion. But now, if I may say it, came the sensation of the day by my executing one of those 'famous runs' which people speak of to this day. I took the ball the whole length of the field, passed four men and eluding all opponents, kicked and scored. This achievement is added to the list of 'Archie's big runs' which it seems footballers are in the habit of recalling whenever they meet to talk of Villa victories.

"Against such a team as the Albion the performance was considered almost phenomenal. Thus the game ended and at last we had had the satisfaction of defeating our tough opponents by four to one.

"Among the Albion players I should like to mention F. Bunn, half-back. He was commonly called 'Little Bunny' and was a smart player of rather small dimensions. I fancy I can hear now the shout of the crowd: 'Look out, Archie, Bunny's coming,' for this player had got a habit of running up and half-noticed, taking the ball from me. I scarcely know how he did it; he seemed to be able to run through my legs and when he had stolen up unawares I usually found the leather missing.

"On this day the Villa men were all in good fettle and Albert Brown, among others, distinguished himself time after time. As for Bunn, his pretty little trick failed altogether and the first time he tried it on he was thrown down and so great was his collapse that, as one of the spectators said at the time, his friends 'had to get picks and shovels to get him out again.' It was a grand, exciting game from beginning to end and speaking for myself, I scarcely remember ever feeling in better form. For my part I had made up my mind to put forth all I knew to win and no one could take the ball from me that day. The same spirit was manifest in all the other players and though the Albion played a sturdy and gallant game, it is not too much to say that we thoroughly overplayed them and towards the end of the game they seemed to lose heart.

"Having thus asserted ourselves once more we took a beating from Preston North End the following week with a good grace. The North End were at that time playing excellently and few there were who could compete successfully with them. We had already experienced one reverse at their hands and as we had to travel to Preston we scarcely hoped to turn the tables upon them. The day turned out to be gusty and we only took ten men including three of the second eleven. Up to half-time the game was pretty even, but after that we were overpowered completely."

"Who were the best men on the other side, Mr. Hunter?"

"Gordon, Ross senior and Ross junior, Drummond and Dewhurst, all of whom played a magnificent game. They are all playing still, except Ross junior, who has been debarred by an accident and Dewhurst. They scored seven goals to our two.

"On May 2nd we resumed our contests for the Mayor's Cup. Three times it had fallen to our lot to meet the Walsall Swifts in the final tie and the games had always been exciting and productive of good scientific play. The weather was fine, but the sun was rather fierce and we started with the disadvantage of having to play with it in our eyes.

"After the first quarter of an hour, however, we kept up a persistent attack upon the Swifts' stronghold, but were forced to retreat before the strong defence offered by the Swifts' backs. Our shooting was not so accurate as it should have been, partly owing to the dazzling light, but at half-time neither side had scored. During the latter half of the game great determination was displayed by both teams and it was not until the Walsall contingent had scored that we fully realised what a great effort was demanded of us. We were most desirous of not losing the Cup for the first time since it had been competed for and through the instrumentality of Whateley a draw was effected.

"A little ill-feeling was displayed towards the end of the game and the officials had to interfere, but this may be forgiven when the excited state of feelings is taken into consideration.

"We had to go to Walsall three weeks later to play off and fortunately, though it was late in May, the day was not particularly warm. Again we had a hard fight and there is no mistake that the Swifts fought well. In fact, I think the Villa were a bit lucky that they managed to again obtain a draw, each side scoring once.

"It was decided not to play for an extra half-hour, as someone suggested and in the end the Association agreed to engrave the names of both the teams upon the shield and each club held the trophy in turn for the season, until it was competed for again. Such was the rather novel termination to a prolonged and exciting contest."

"And so ended the 1884-5 season, I presume?"

"Yes. But there is another match to which I ought to refer, which was played between the Villa and the Preston North End on May 9th. The North End came down to Perry Barr and considered purely from the sporting point of view, the game was an excellent one. We were only too pleased to arrange for the visit, for a desire had been expressed in many quarters to have an opportunity of seeing the noted club in Birmingham.

"The fixture was hailed with satisfaction and a good crowd was drawn to witness the proceedings, in spite of the boisterous weather. A cordial greeting awaited the visitors and it was soon seen that the Villa were playing a weaker game than their opponents.

"The game does not call for much description, though I cannot avoid mentioning that for the first time we had to find fault with our goal-keeper, who seemed either unable or unwilling to defend his charge. Indeed, we and the spectators, were very wroth with Harvey, who was by no means playing up to his usual form; but even if he had been we should have had little chance of winning the match. Finally we were defeated by five goals to none.

"The visit of the North End is memorable, however, for other reasons than these and after this lapse of time I can give a dispassionate account of what happened without, I hope, hurting anybody's feelings. One of our players had been kicked and in the heat of the moment he retaliated upon his opponent. The officials intervened and the incident might have ended there and been satisfactorily explained afterwards if the crowd had not interfered and aroused angry feelings at the end of the game.

"When the Preston team were leaving the field a number of roughs gathered round them and charged them with using their weight unfairly. Of course, the charge was indignantly denied, but the denial only exasperated the crowd the more and free fights could be seen taking place all over the field. After dressing, the team prepared to depart, but to our dismay we found an excited and rough gathering round the tent and the appearance of the Preston men was the signal for the renewal of the quarrel. The hostile demonstration continued until the visitors had departed and left a very bad impression upon everybody's mind.

"The Preston team not unnaturally were offended, but they freed the Villa Committee of all responsibility and in after-times new fixtures were made which had none of these unpleasant details."

"Are such incidents common, Mr. Hunter?"

"So far as Birmingham is concerned, certainly not," Archie replied, "and my experience is that they are very exceptional elsewhere. The spectators are usually good judges of the game and appreciative of good play and though their sympathies are, as might only be expected, strongly with the local team, they are generally pretty fair to both sides. I only remember one other case of importance where a hostile feeling was provoked and was likely to lead to a breach of the peace.

"I played in a match when one of the members of the opposing team played a merciless game from beginning to end and he ended up by crippling Howard Vaughton. Then the spectators could stand it no longer and we were obliged to form a bodyguard and escort the obnoxious player from the field and take him to a neighbouring house. Even here, however, he was not safe. The people stormed the place and the frightened man was forced to take to flight. He got out at the back, scaled several walls and then made off by unfrequented ways, thus avoiding the violence with which he was threatened.

"Our own committee always did their best to guard against incidents of this character and were usually successful; but of course, they could not restrain a crowd of several thousands. At Walsall once the Villa team was mobbed and we had to run the gauntlet at Chuckery Grounds."

"And now, Mr. Hunter, I shall be glad to hear something of the 1885-6 season."

"Certainly," said Archie. "You will observe by the table I have here that the 1885-6 season showed an improvement upon the previous one and enabled our supporters to anticipate some of the great achievements which marked the following year and resulted in the Villa taking a pre-eminent position in the football world. The following is the record:-

Season 1885-6.

Matches	played	59
	won	32
	lost	20
	drawn	7
Goals	gained	177
	lost	94

We did not begin well. At Blackburn we met the Rovers on September 26th and were defeated by two goals to one. The two teams were pretty equal, but the odds were against us in having to travel – a factor of some importance with the Villa, as is still evident in these days.

"The following week the Halliwell team paid their first visit to the Midlands and we decisively beat them by six goals to nil. Their two backs, Robb and Bone, played well, but otherwise the performance of the team made but a slight impression upon the spectators.

"Following on this we encountered Derby County, who were at that time a promising club just coming into notice. Afterwards when they introduced some Scotch players into the team they did excellent work and took a high position. Among their members they counted the two Shiltons, now playing for Notts County and 'Little Morley' the back, was a good exponent of the game. He also went to Notts County afterwards. I think the Derby club was at its best in 1888 and 1889 and the assistance which they received from Spilsbury doubtless did much to help them to take a foremost place.

"On the first occasion of our meeting the County we defeated them by four goals to two, but the aspect of things was entirely changed when we met them again on November 16th. Spilsbury was present on that occasion and was of immense assistance to his side and we, on the other hand, had our left wing palpably weak. We were defeated by two goals to none, to the great disappointment of the supporters who had followed us over.

"I remember a curious feature of the game. One of the Derby half-backs seemed to have had instructions to keep a special watch on me and he nobly fulfilled his task. Though he did nothing with the ball himself he dogged me wherever I went and could not be shaken off. He at all events succeeded in his mission, for I could never play the ball and feed the forwards. Whenever the ball was near me he came along and charged and knocked me off it, so that, take it altogether, I had not a very pleasant afternoon. People talk about being 'shadowed'. That has been my fate more than once, though I am glad to say it has only been in friendly rivalry on the football field."

Chapter 16

More About the 1885-6 Season

"You have already learnt," said Archie Hunter, "what an ambitious club Aston Villa were and we were very anxious indeed to win the English Cup. This, of course, was a matter of time, but we kept the idea foremost and gradually worked up to the crowning triumph.

"The antagonism associated with the English Cup ties in the Midland counties was always of the most stubborn character and year after year the encounters excited the keenest interest among the sport-loving public. About the middle of October 1885, Aston Villa and Walsall Town met in the first round of the competition for the coveted trophy at The Chuckery, Walsall. The weather was dull and uninviting, but the match was well patronised. I have given you plenty of examples, I think, of the rivalry existing between the Black Country clubs and ourselves, but this year that rivalry had been heightened owing to the Villa having obtained three of Walsall's best players.

"Both teams, it was evident from the first, were determined to make a bold bid for supremacy and it was rather expected that the game might become rough, but on the whole we had not so much trouble as we were prepared for. Cox, the present Villa captain, was playing back for Walsall and a moderately strong team was placed in the field. But the luck was all on our side and before five minutes had passed I registered the first point for the Villa and a few minutes later Albert Brown scored again. Walsall then had several good tries at scoring and kept Hobson, our goal, busy; all their attacks were repelled and ultimately we left the field winners by five goals to nil.

"Play, I should add, had to be suspended owing to the spectators breaking over the ground and refusing to return to their places. So far as the national trophy was concerned, however, we had no further chance and were obliged to confine our attentions to the Mayor's Charity Cup.

"A week later we met Notts Forest, playing them upon a ground which was new to us and which had the disadvantage of being soft. This club was playing a very good game at the time and continued to do so until some of the old players dropped out, when it became weaker, but the club still holds a good place.

"The Forest won the toss and pressed us hard from the beginning of the game. At half-time neither side had scored and during the second-half the Forest had the advantage. Repeated shots at goal were made, but without definite result and finally a draw was recorded, no goals being scored on either side.

"On November 7th we played a friendly match with a newly-formed team representing Gloucester County. They came over to Birmingham, but one of the papers remarked that 'their play was more a source of amusement to the spectators than anything else, inasmuch as they seemed entirely at sea when in possession of the ball.' But every allowance should be made for this. In the first place the Association game was not in vogue in Gloucestershire and the players were all fresh to the rules and had had little opportunity of practising."

"Was Dr. W. G. Grace among the players?"

"No, although we had hoped to have an opportunity of seeing the Cricket Champion between the sticks. Dr. Grace had just about this time commenced to take an active interest in Association Football and his name is now on the list of Football League referees. He occasionally played goal, although I do not know of any important match in which he took part. We were very disappointed that he did not give us a chance of seeing him in a new role in Birmingham, where he would have been certain of a popular demonstration. But I scarcely expect that even the sturdy doctor would have been able to change the issue of the game, considering the merits of the other players, for we won the match by eleven goals to one."

"It was not often that you got these easy victories, I suppose?"

"No, very seldom now. One of the next matches we played was of the most exciting description. It came round to our turn to meet our old friends the West Bromwich Albion again and remembering our past experiences, we were prepared for a close fight. Directly after the kick-off the Albion ran the ball rapidly through our goal, but the point was disallowed as being off-side. Ten minutes later, however, they got the ball through again and they continued to have the best of the game, for at half-time the score stood – Albion 2, Villa 0.

"On restarting we did better, but the Albion continued to increase their score and finally won the game by five goals to four. It was a well-contested match, as the finish shows, although nothing very brilliant was done that afternoon by individual players. You may mention 'Darkie' Timmings, however, one of the Albion half-backs, who did an immense amount of work and was of great assistance to his team. He broke his leg a short time ago in the course of the match, but is now, I believe, playing again.

"We next met Burnley, the encounter ending in a draw, each side scoring one goal. The ground was in a fearfully bad condition, a fact which militated against good sport and the game throughout was of the tamest description. The Burnley team was a strong one and with Triel as centre forward capable of playing well.

"In a match against the Blackburn Rovers on December 19th we had a stroke of bad luck, for we were obliged, owing to a storm which raged, to stop playing just as we were beginning to press our opponents hard. They had scored three times to our once in the early part of the game, so we were obliged to put up with the defeat. The Rovers worked hard for victory and it must not be begrudged them. They executed some brilliant runs and played with dash and determination throughout.

"Some compensation was afforded us a week later when we defeated Acton, a London organisation by Thirteen to one. This was one of four matches which we had arranged to play during the Christmas holidays – three with London clubs and one with the second eleven of Queen's Park. Acton was rather off colour and was, moreover, but a young club, so perhaps we ought not to take too much credit for our achievement.

Arthur Brown scored four goals, Whateley four, Allen three and Burton and I one each.

"Our next match was the London Scottish, which was played in a tempest. Owing to the severity of the weather, the first half only lasted just over half an hour, during which time we had scored two goals and our opponents none. Immediately upon the resumption of play we added a third point, then Burton added a fourth, Whateley a fifth and Allen a sixth and seventh. So you see it was altogether a one-sided affair and I doubt whether the spectators who ran the risk of being thoroughly drenched with rain were much repaid for their discomfort.

"The third match of the series was played under no happier conditions. Our opponents were the London Casuals and they were a very different team to deal with to those we had met before. The ground was covered with snow and it was difficult to play an accurate game. After we had scored two points the Casuals rallied and played vigorously. Dr. Smith obtained their first goal and we retaliated by again sending the ball through the posts; but the Doctor returned to the attack and speedily scored again. We then forced the visitors to play a defensive game, but at length a sharp run by Dr. Smith took the Villa backs by surprise. Before they could frustrate his progress the doctor was well up the field. Hobson, not very judiciously, came some distance out of goal and ran towards him. The doctor was now on the right hand side of the goal posts and a capital opportunity was afforded the Casuals to score. The doctor was well aware of this and promptly centred the ball to Hurst, left wing and the leather was dexterously sent through the posts, there being no custodian to stop it. This proved to be the winning point for the Casuals, for at the end of the game the score still stood:- Villa 3, Casuals 4."

"And now what about the work of the new year, Mr. Hunter?"

"Well," said Archie, "we began very well by beating Aston Unity by five goals to nil. The following week the weather was so wretched that very few matches were played in the Midlands and we were obliged to abandon a fixture with Nottingham Jardines.

"On January 16th we encountered Accrington again and by dint of hard work we obtained a victory of two goals to nil. We next beat the Excelsior, a fairly strong team, by three goals to nil and then came another momentous tussle with the West Bromwich Albion, who had, only a fortnight before, beaten the Old Carthusians in the English Cup tie. We were anxious to wipe off the stigma of the last defeat, one of a long series, but it was in vain.

"The Albion were in splendid condition and although they had to keep themselves in reserve for the sixth round of the English Cup the following Saturday, they were able to defeat us by three goals to two. It was a stiff contest and some excellent play was shown on both sides. The following week, I may mention, the Albion were again in such fit form that they defeated the Old Westminsters by six goals to nil.

"The same day we were engaged in playing Notts County again and we won by five to three. Meeting Oxford University a week later we scored another victory of three goals to nil against classical players.

"We were beaten by Burnley, however, the following week (two to one) and we next drew with the Wolverhampton Wanderers and Derby County. So far, as you will observe from this hasty summary, affairs had been unexciting, but in April we met the Notts Rangers in the first round of ties for the Mayor of Birmingham's Charity Cup and this gave to our matches a higher interest. We won by five goals to one and then came the best game of the season, our opponents being the Queen's Park.

"As regards the visiting team I should explain that at the last moment it was found that some of the usual members would not be able to keep their engagement, but in order to save us disappointment a team was made up consisting of five Queen's Park men and the rest from other prominent Scotch clubs. They were all excellent exponents of the game and the play at times was extremely fast and hot. The visitors played a splendid defensive game, Watson in particular extricating the ball from several dangerous scrimmages in front of the Scotch citadel. We had the best of the game in the earlier part and just before half-time secured the first point.

"On resuming the visitors steadily bore down upon our goal and the ball was presently headed through. With the score equal each side played a careful but determined game and runs by the forwards of both teams were frequent. Queen's Park then began to get the advantage and Snedden headed the ball right into goal. Ashmore, our custodian saved, but Snedden again sent it in and this time the shot told. As nothing further accrued the visitors won by two to one.

"In the evening the two teams dined together under the chairmanship of Mr. H. Gilzean-Reid, who was then the parliamentary representative of Aston. In proposing the toast of the guests Mr. Reid spoke in flattering terms of both the teams and said he thought Aston Villa had done a great deal towards raising the standard of football and had given the game a tone and position which was new in the history of the sport. Mr. Rowan, the captain, replied and thus a pleasant visit was pleasantly ended.

"In connection with the Mayor's Cup, we defeated Aston Unity in May by seven goals to nil. The final tie was played off on Monday, May 17th, our opponents being the Wednesbury Old Athletics. The weather was inclement and a strong wind materially interfered with the play. At first there was plenty of hard work to do, but in the end we proved more than a match for the 'Old Uns' and won by four goals to one and we consequently obtained possession of the Cup for the year.

"So ended the season, which on the whole, was a quiet one, but I have given you the details in order that the history of the club may be complete.

"I have now only a few words to say as to the season which followed, when we reached the high-water mark of success. It was in the 1886-7 season that Mr. George Ramsay, the first Villa captain, became our manager. In that season we practically carried everything before us.

"I wish to reserve all details for a fresh chapter, but in order to indicate the importance of what has at last to be told I may as well give you the season's record, which I think you will agree is in every way remarkable:-

151

Season 1886-7

Matches	played	56
	Won	44
	Tied	8
	Lost	4
Goals	gained	223
	lost	62

With these figures before you, you will be prepared for a story of many victories, culminating in the triumph for which every football club hopes, the winning of the English Cup."

Chapter 17

In Training for the English Cup

"Now Mr. Hunter are you ready to fight the battles of 1886-7 over again?" I asked as I sat down for a chat with the Villa captain.

Archie's eyes brightened at the prospect, for what footballer does not know all that the 1886-7 season meant to Aston Villa? In the history of every club a cup year means an epoch. There is no danger of forgetting it, or the train of circumstances leading up to the achievement. The story is told again and again and repetition burnishes the memory and keeps the facts vivid and unobliterated in spite of time. Archie entered upon his narrative without hesitation and told the story of the year as if he were accustomed to the recital.

"The history of the 1886-7 season," he said, "is the history of much hard work, some exciting struggles and many victories. Our record I have already given you and you will have observed that we only lost four matches out of the fifty-six played, only one of those four was of any importance. The West Bromwich Albion knocked us out in the first round of the Birmingham Cup Tie and that, of course, was a reverse which we felt; but the remaining three defeats were not in connection with events of much consideration. Our teams this year had undergone some changes and it was just at this time that the professional element was being introduced. Some of the old members, myself among the number, who had been playing as amateurs, had a great reluctance to be paid for our services. Our diffidence may or may not have been reasonable, but it was sincere. When we finally ceased to be amateurs I may say that we left it entirely with the committee to arrange terms; and I never have much sympathy with players who put pecuniary conditions first and think of the sport afterwards. But professionalism is so strong and competition for good players so great that a 'pro' may ask for a good round sum as a retaining fee in addition to a high salary and stand every chance of obtaining both.

"A good member of our team whom we missed this season was Eli Davis, who had taken part in so many of our encounters and shared with us all our varying experiences. We had some difficulty at first in getting a successor to him. Our attention had been directed to a very promising young player named Loach, who had distinguished himself while a member of the West Bromwich Albion. He was considered one of their best forwards and was induced to join the Villa. In the first two matches in which he took part he played well and we had great hopes of him, but afterwards he sprained his knee and fell off and had ultimately to be replaced. One of our new members, who is still playing well, was Freddy Dawson, a capital centre half-back. One or two more new names will be introduced as we get further into the season.

"I may also mention that this year the leopards changed their spots – or rather, the Villa changed their colours, which is, perhaps, a simpler matter. In November we decided to put aside the piebald uniform, which was inartistic and never popular and we donned in its place the light blue and cardinal vertically-striped jerseys which afterwards became so well known. There was another advantage in the change of colours. The old uniform was associated with some notable reverses and we were determined, if possible, in this season to turn over a new leaf and alter everything for the better. Our first fixture was a friendly match with the Welsh Druids, a fairly good team, who offered a stubborn resistance to us, but were lacking in combination."

"What is your opinion of Welsh teams, Mr. Hunter?"

"Of Welsh teams I have not a very high opinion," Archie replied. "They are inferior either to English or Scotch, but there are many individual players who deserve to be ranked among the best exponents of the game. When a Welshman gets into a thoroughly good club he is usually very serviceable, but there never seems to be a sufficient number of good players to make up a strong team composed exclusively of Welshmen. The Druids, in 1886, were considered a promising club and they counted several good players among their members. We arranged to play them because we were anxious to get a connection in Wales, but the Druids did not continue their good form and after a season or two we did not meet them again. Our first match ended in the Villa defeating them by 5 to 0, and it was in this encounter that Loach played for us for the first time and did remarkably well. Just a year later, I may as well mention here, we met the Druids again and a rather loosely-played but fast game ended in our winning by 4 to 2. We decided the following Monday to carry out a new idea so far as we were concerned, although the custom prevails in Scotland and that was to have a match between 'Probables' and 'Improbables' of the Villa team."

"What do you mean by that, Mr. Hunter?"

"Simply this. We wanted to test the capability of every individual member of the team and so we had a trial match, twelve players being selected from among the junior members and the usual first team. I captained the 'Probables' and R. Dawson the 'Improbables' and though the match ended, as we all expected, in a big victory for the 'Probables' we were able to pick out some likely 'colts' and distinguish the most promising players, who had hitherto had no chance of making their merits known. If I were asked for an opinion I should strongly recommend this system as it not infrequently is an advantage to a committee and gives a fair chance to a promising young player to have his good points recognised.

"After this our season may be said to have properly opened with a friendly match against the Sheffield Wednesday on October 2nd. I remember it chiefly because it was what I call one of my days out. I seemed to do pretty well what I liked and with the help of my colleagues I was able to take advantage of every point and time after time I made rings round the Sheffield backs and scored easily. We were all in a happy mood that afternoon and I remember that as we left the field the spectators burst into spontaneous cheering. We had beaten Sheffield Wednesday by seven to nil. Dennis Hodgetts, one of our new men, played well, but a critic of the game wrote that 'Archie was the hero of the match and out of the seven goals scored, placed four of them to his own credit – doing the whole trick himself, trotting in and out of the Sheffield forwards with the greatest ease and finally sending the ball through'."

"Do you know why the Sheffield team is called the Wednesday?"

"Yes. It was the custom of the club to play its matches on that day; that is all."

"What was your next match?"

"I must speak of it with bated breath," said Archie. "We met West Bromwich Albion in the first round for the Birmingham Cup and there was the usual excitement as to the result. The Albion were at this time remarkably strong and every member of the team was a picked player capable of excellent work. Starting with the goalkeeper, 'Bobby' Roberts, I don't think there was a finer goalkeeper in the three kingdoms. He was, I am firmly convinced, the mainstay of the team. It was a marvellous shot that he could not stop and the man who got the better of 'Bobby' was extraordinarily clever. The Albion would not have achieved the triumphs it did if Roberts had been missing. I used to speak of him as their salvation, for when all the other players were equally matched, Roberts' superiority just turned the scale in the favour of his own team. He is still playing and last season joined Sunderland, but we are soon to see him again in his old position between the posts for West Bromwich Albion. May he do as well again for them as he did of old.

"Then there was Green, who played back, a faithful and hard worker, who was particularly sure in defence. James Bayliss, the captain, was a splendid centre forward and Charlie Perry was hard to beat as a centre half-back. But there:- you may as well mention the lot of them – Aldridge, Horton, Timmins, Woodhall, Holden, Paddock, Pearson and Wilson – for they were indeed a fine set of fellows and in combination almost irresistible. As you know they had defeated the Villa time after time, although once or twice we had shown ourselves more than a match for them. We had now to try conclusions with them once more and for the Birmingham Cup too! Well, you may take it for granted that nobody expected an easy or a one-sided game and in this expectation nobody was disappointed.

"As we had to play the Albion on their own ground, it added to their chances and I may mention that we had never won on the Stoney Lane ground. Nor did we this time. The battle waged furiously; we put forth all our strength and did all we knew; we gave the Albion some hard work also. They rushed the leather through after five minutes' play, but they never had another chance all afternoon. Greek had met Greek and no mistake. The Albion combination was seen to great advantage. Wherever the ball was, there were two or three men ready for all emergencies. Whenever one of our team obtained possession of the ball he was pounced upon and fairly forced to leave it. Instructions had been given, I have been told, for the West Bromwich men to 'keep an eye on Archie' and I had never a chance. Loach, who was playing against his old club, failed to show to advantage, though some excuse can be found for him. The gate, I may add, made a record for the district, for 20,000 spectators were on the ground. Imagine if you can the ear-splitting cheer they sent up when the Albion scored and when they left the field winners of the game. At one portion of the game the barriers gave way and one man was very seriously injured. Yes," Archie continued, "it was a memorable day and the better team won. The Albion had entered upon one of the biggest seasons and their all-round play was a wonder to behold. Later on in the season, but I had better reserve that, hadn't I? Let us get on to the next match."

"Whom did you meet?"

"Notts Rangers and the Villa won by 7 to 0. I was not present at the match and Freddy Dawson captained the team. It may strike you as a curious point, but although I am always spoken of as being the Villa captain at the time, I had not been formally appointed to the position. It was well understood that when I was on the ground I should captain the team, but practically I was elected every week and when I was absent some other member was appointed – anyone on whom the team decided at the time. This is still a custom in some clubs and it has its advantages, I dare say. Well, after the Rangers we met the Wednesbury Old Athletics in the first round of the English Cup tie and owing to the weakness of our opponents, the match aroused very little interest. The feature of the match was the bad goalkeeping on the Wednesbury side. Our opponents lost their spirits in an early part of the game and when we had scored seven or eight times with the greatest ease the goalkeeper was removed, but we continued to add to our points and eventually left the field winners by thirteen to none. It was, on the whole, a melancholy affair, especially when we recalled our first gigantic struggles with the 'Old Uns' and remembered how 15,000 hardy Black Country allies had come over to see them beat the Villa."

"Tempora mutantur" I murmured feelingly and Archie silently signified his agreement.

"A friendly match with the Wolverhampton Wanderers followed and we defeated them by five goals to one," Archie continued. "The Wanderers were only just beginning and were not a very strong organisation. But they were destined to take the position which Stafford Road were vacating.

"The Villa next defeated Middlesbrough by 8 to 1 and then came the second round in the cup tie, our opponents being the Derby Midland. This team was also on the decline and the Derby County were coming to the fore. Formerly the Derby Midland were the crack team of Derbyshire, but Derby County had been strong enough the previous season to knock us out of the competition. We had really lost that match through being too sure of it and consequently careless. We beat the Derby Midland by six goals to one, after a spirited game. People now began to have great hopes of us and someone wrote:- 'Were it not for the 'bright star' of the North, many would back the Villa to win the Cup.' It is a curious coincidence that on the day we defeated Derby Midland, West Bromwich Albion disposed of Derby Junction and Mitchell's St. George's of Derby County, so that on that day the Derbyites might well cry 'Ichabod' for the glory had departed from them. All these matches were in connection with the second round of the National Cup, too, which made the disaster for Derbyshire the greater. Our supporters, however, might well be hopeful, for up to this time we had played altogether twenty-one matches, of which we had won 17; lost 3 and drawn 1. We had gained 94 goals and lost 18. Not a bad record, was it?

"We met the Stafford Rangers and played in semi-darkness. The play was wild and reckless at times, everybody kicking the ball about in a half-aimless sort of way. At the top goal quite a little illumination proceeded from a number of youths holding up lighted wax matches. This excited so much ridicule that the whistle was blown and the game ended abruptly.

"Our quarterly meeting was held soon afterwards, when it was found that the Villa stood first on the list of football clubs with an average of 4.85 goals to one. The Preston North End came second with 4.84 to one and the West Bromwich Albion third with 4.81 to one. With the exception of the Bolton Wanderers, the Villa had also played more matches than any other club. Some of our members had met with misfortunes during the season, however. Albert Brown received a nasty knock on the head when playing at Derby and Dennis Hodgetts and Yates also met with mishaps which prevented them from playing for a while.

"After one or two unimportant matches we came to the third round in the cup tie, our opponents being the Wolverhampton Wanderers, who showed unexpected good form. The game was rough but brilliant and when I say rough I do not mean that it was ill-natured so much as it was stubborn and fiercely contested with a view to victory. Many times the players might be seen sprawling on the ground, the result of some terrific charge or knockdown blow; and shortly before half-time Burton was noticed running off the field with blood streaming down his face. It appeared that he had come into violent contact with someone else's head, but fortunately his injuries appeared to be much worse than they really were. In short, the game was more like a war than anything else I can think of and this was doubtless due to the eagerness with which each side entered upon the contest. Two of our goals were disallowed and the game was ultimately left drawn, each side scoring two points. A fog was rapidly coming on when time was called and opinion was much divided as to whether we should play on an extra half-hour or not. Finally, to settle the matter, we tossed up, but the continuance of the game left the issue undecided. Some capital play was seen, especially in the second part of the proceedings and the two goalkeepers carried off equal honours.

"The last match of the year was with the Albion. The day was intensely cold and everybody pitied the goalkeepers, who were nearly frozen. At half-time the Albion had scored once and we had not managed to score at all and the game nearly to its close looked like another win for our agile opponents. Albert Brown, however, put in a splendid centre from which Vaughton was able to score and the game ended in a draw.

"We began the new year with a match against the Hibernians, played at Edinburgh and ended in a victory for us by eight to three. Our second team, the same day, beat the second team of Queen's Park by two goals to one in what is known as the 'sliding match,' the ground being in such a state that the players could not run, but were obliged to 'slether' to the ball. While in Scotland our first team met Queen's Park at Glasgow and in pouring rain we succeeded in defeating the veterans by five goals to one. The spectators were much enraged at the result and we had experience of what a disappointed mob can do. They tore down the goalposts and fences and smashed the pay boxes and a riot was only prevented from getting serious by the timely appearance on the scene of a large force of police.

"Then came the second tussle with the Wolverhampton Wanderers in the Cup tie. They were now more popularly known as the 'Wolves' and again we drew with them, only one goal being registered on either side. The Wanderers had been steadily training for the contest for three weeks and their back division was particularly strong and efficient. Griffiths, the goalkeeper, also played gamely and saved his charge many times. Our forwards played a passing game in their best style and had it not been for the miserable weather a very pretty exposition of the scientific game would have been seen. The play started briskly and somewhat to our consternation had not proceeded long before the Wanderers scored out of a scrimmage. We equalised after a vigorous effort and then the toughest part of the contest began, each side working its hardest. The ball could be seen bobbing up and down the field at a tremendous pace, the teams in hot pursuit and full of excitement. But no other goals were scored.

"Again we tried conclusions with the team and when we trooped on to the field we could see that the spectators were intensely excited as to the result. Our own feelings you can also judge of a little when you remember all that victory meant. At half-time the score stood – Wanderers one, Villa none. So far the play had been sharp and at times rough, the referee having in one case to severely reprimand one of the 'Wolves'. Nerving ourselves and getting ready for a special effort we entered upon the second part of the game and out of a scrimmage we rushed the ball through. Encouraged by this success we pressed our opponents hard and in less than five minutes Brown found a weak spot and scored a second goal for us. We decided then to play strictly on the defensive and up to five minutes of 'time' it seemed certain that this third battle was to be decisive and that the Villa were to be the victors. But the 'Wolves' were not yet going to despair and with a fine combined rush they got the ball through and again equalised matters. In the hope of terminating this prolonged struggle we decided to play an extra half-hour and we speedily added another point to our record. But the Wanderers followed this up and for the third time Aston Villa and Wolverhampton Wanderers drew, three goals each being registered.

"Shall I go on and tell you how this struggle ended? No, I think I may safely leave it for a new chapter, for there is much to tell."

Chapter 18

The Tug of War

Three times had the Wolverhampton Wanderers and Aston Villa faced one another and three times had the issue been left undecided. Each club so far could show a good record and it was almost impossible for the critics to venture upon predicting which side would ultimately prove supreme.

"As you already know, we had been drawn together in the third round and on December 11th played our first match in the Cup tie. A draw ensued, each side scoring two goals, although two other goals scored by us were disallowed on technical grounds. Probably we underestimated our opponents at the first meeting, but at the second we felt pretty confident of winning. Our opponents, however, were tough and this time we only scored one goal each. The third encounter took place on January 22nd and caused some dissatisfaction by the fact that the Association did not order the match to be replayed either on neutral ground or at Perry Barr. Another draw was added to the remarkable record and thus on January 29th we once more found ourselves face to face with the 'Wolves'.

"The crowd to see the match was an enormous one and ranks among the biggest ever known on our ground. Vehicles of all kinds from the coach of the local M.P. (Mr. George Kynoch, who was one of the Villa's warmest supporters) to the humble one-horse shay, surrounded the meadow; and all round the ropes the surging multitude stood, swaying backwards and forwards in their intense anxiety to obtain a glimpse of the play. The roof of a neighbouring shed was crowded with ardent (but non-paying) sightseers and some trees in the vicinity afforded a coign of vantage to dozens more.

"The players, on entering the field, were warmly cheered. We had been in steady training for the event and every Villan looked as if he meant that day to do his utmost to win. We won the toss and played downhill.

"Amid a hum of excitement the game began by Brodie kicking off. The ball was worked to the front and then Coulton removed the pressure and Dawson took the ball into the Wanderers' quarters. A corner fell to us and the ball was sent over the Wanderers' goalline. At this point Brodie retired for a while, having been hurt. Then I got the chance of a shot, but the ball was returned. Dawson secured it and amid tremendous enthusiasm scored the first goal within ten minutes of the start. A hot scrimmage in goal followed and it was with difficulty we cleared our lines. Brodie, returning amid encouraging cheers then got to work and our goalkeeper was kept busy.

"Getting possession again, we persistently attacked the Wanderers' stronghold; and at last Brown passed to me and with a clean shot I again lowered the visitors' colours. The game so far had been very fast; now it slowed down somewhat, but Griffiths, the Wolverhampton goalkeeper, had plenty to do and covered himself with glory time after time. At half-time the score still remained – Villa 2, Wanderers 0.

"On changing ends our rivals at once rushed the ball into our territory, but they did not succeed in scoring. The game warmed up again; exciting runs, attack and counter-attack, hot shots and smart passing were quite the order of the day and the enthusiasm of the spectators was aroused to the highest pitch. As time went on and no other point was gained, we could hear our supporters shouting heartily, 'Get another, Villa,' but when the game was over and we were declared finally the winners in this prolonged struggle, nothing could restrain the crowd from rushing across the field and making one of those demonstrations which were more pleasant to the feelings than comforting to the senses.

"Everyone agreed that the Wanderers, though defeated, had come out of the encounter with the highest honours of war. Their play, especially that of the back division, was excellent and Mason, Griffiths, Baugh and Lowder were simply invaluable to the team. Brodie's accident handicapped them, although he worked hard and well. It was generally considered that the Villa displayed on this occasion more than their customary dash and all the players came in for personal compliments. Thus ended one of the most notable of our struggles and our victory of course led to much speculation as to our future chances. We had never before reached a higher stage in the competition for the Cup than the fourth round, but now our friends began to hope that at least we should have a place in the semi-final, for which also Preston North End, Glasgow Rangers and West Bromwich Albion were favourites. Our chance of winning the trophy itself was considered rather remote, Preston North End and the Albion being put before the Villa."

"What was your own idea, Mr. Hunter?"

"Well, I had a lurking suspicion," said Archie guardedly, "that we might do the trick ourselves, but that might have been vanity."

"You had good reason for your opinion, I suppose?"

"Certainly. The team was in splendid fettle and had never shown better ability. We worked well together and made a strong feature of our combination. The smart runs of the forwards, the tackling of the backs and the hard kicking of all the team were spoken of by all the experts; and looking at what we had done I felt pretty confident of what we yet could do. So far as the Albion was concerned it had hitherto proved itself our superior, but only very slightly. Preston North End, too, had defeated us; yet we venture to hope on turning the tables upon such formidable antagonists as they. Courage is half the battle, people say and at least we had the courage. The result will tell you whether it was justified or not."

"Whom did you meet in the next round?"

"Horncastle, a team which did not trouble us much," said Archie. "The game was a poor one, although one or two of the visitors were first-class players. We had the best of the play throughout and were not often called upon to defend and the result of persistent attacking on our part was that we won by five goals to nil. One of our team at this time, whom I do not think I have told you of, was Frank Coulton, who came from

Mitchell's St. George's. He was a very strong back, with any amount of pluck and a tremendous power of kicking. He would watch his man like a cat and then pounce upon him and send the ball spinning far away. Just now he is out of the team, suffering that disaster which is so common to footballers – a sprained knee.

"On February 12th it fell to our lot to meet Darwen and a very fine and close encounter was the result. This was the most important team we had met during the season, for the Darwen had a splendid record and had twice figured in the semi-final for the National Cup. In the first-half we pressed our opponents very hard and scored three times. The number would have been doubled had it not been for Hugh McIntyre, late of the Blackburn Rovers, who on this occasion, played goal for Darwen. He had given up playing in mid-field and had been asked by Darwen to join them, but no one could conceive that in a new position he could display such extraordinary powers. He was the most distinguished player that day, saving many a scorching shot and returning the ball in a way that simply amazed us. He was cheered all over the field for his grand display of goalkeeping and there is no doubt that but for him we should have had an easier and more decisive victory.

"In the second part of the game our play fell off and our supporters were full of anxiety lest the Darwen should exceed the score we had already made. They gained two points in quick succession, but failed to equalise and thus victory remained with us.

"At half-time the Rugby Cup was put on the field and filled with champagne by Mr. Amos Roe and during the interval each of the players was invited to drink a little of the exhilarating beverage.

"Take it for all in all it was a dashing game on both sides. McIntyre's phenomenal dexterity was displayed at a very early period, but out of a scrimmage Dawson sent in a long swift shot so speedy that Hugh was fairly beaten. Warner, on our side, was pretty idle during the first part of the game and in the second half he allowed the Darwen team to get their first goal quite easily. He was rather nervous, too. Little Joey Simmonds's tackling of the right wing of the visitors was, however, a special feature of the game; and as regards the Villa forwards a critic wrote:- 'They worked with such capital combination that it is difficult to select one more than another for special commendation. There was not one among them who did not send in two or three first-rate shots which with any ordinary goalkeeper would have been goals. Archie Hunter was in his old form and marshalled his men with all the experience of the careful general he is. The selfish element was also absent and the manner in which the men passed to one another speaks well for the careful training they have undergone of late.

"The result of the match is very satisfactory and it is to be hoped, for the first time in the history of the club, it will play in the final.' Preston North End, whom we had feared as much as any, had now been defeated by the Blackburn Rovers. So we began to breathe freely. Then West Bromwich Albion defeated Notts County in a magnificent game and on February 26th we played a friendly match with the same club. Having advanced to this stage we now began to think of undergoing special training for the great event which was to follow. You will like to know, I think, how we trained for the English Cup.

"At the end of February we beat Notts County by three to one, all of us playing a very good game that day, which heightened the hopes of our supporters as to our fitness for greater contests. I was in very good form myself, but in the course of the game I got a severe bruise and when it was all over I felt bad.

"We travelled from Nottingham to Birmingham and obtained the necessary apparel for training and went on the same night to Droitwich. Outside the station a brake was waiting for us and on a pitch dark night a dozen of us rode through the quiet country lanes to a little unfrequented place on the river Severn called Holt Fleet.

"Here we arrived at midnight and being tired with the day's exertions and drowsy with the ride, we tumbled off to bed. The hotel accommodation in those days at Holt Fleet was of a limited character and the host was not accustomed to such large parties asking for accommodation. He was not prepared for us and the first night we had to rough it. Six of us slept in a top attic in which three beds had been placed. I say we slept, but this is not quite correct. We were put there to sleep, but the pestilence that stalks by night was opposed to us.

"All this, of course, was remedied later on by the obliging host, who did his utmost to make us comfortable. But you will wonder why we chose this place for our purpose. It was not our discovery, but was recommended to us by W. G. George, the champion mile-runner. It was his custom to walk, when training, from Bromsgrove to Droitwich and Holt Fleet lies between these two places. The district is very favourable for athletes. There is a fine stretch of open country and there is the river, which affords every facility for boating and swimming. Then the walks all around are delightful and the brine baths at Droitwich are, of course, very convenient.

"Since we were there other football teams have experienced its advantages, the Wolverhampton Wanderers in particular. Well, here we stayed for a week with our trainer, 'Billy' Gorman. He was a famous sprint runner and had won a special handicap; and when he ceased to take part in public contests himself he devoted himself to training athletes (George among the number) and a capital fellow he was."

"Will you describe your course of training, Mr. Hunter?"

"We got up each morning at eight o'clock prompt and breakfasted. Afterwards we strolled about as we pleased for an hour or so. Then we put our uniform on and by permission, which was kindly granted by Lord Dudley's overseer, we were allowed the use of the ground behind the hotel for sprint running and long distance running. It was curious to observe the difference which practice speedily made in some or our physical abilities. There was Dennis Hodgetts, for example, who was called our slow man. Up to this time he was indeed lacking in that desirable quality of fastness which is so serviceable on the field. But after this training he wonderfully developed into one of the speediest of the set and was only excelled by Richard Davis (late of the Walsall Swifts) who had the reputation of being the fastest player for short distances. All the others were very quick: Albert Brown, Joey Simmonds, Jack Burton,

Freddy Dawson, Howard Vaughton, Harry Yates and Albert Allen, but the sprint running improved their form tremendously.

"As for me, I went in for long distance running, with Warner our goalkeeper, who had no particular need to go in for this training and Coulton, for my companions. Albert Allen, I should here explain, was our reserve man who was in readiness to take Dawson's place if necessary, for Freddy had seriously hurt his knee and we were very uncertain whether he would be able to play. However, when the right time came the question was put to all the team and they decided that he was fit, so Allen was not needed after all.

"Well, so the morning went. Sometimes the team walked along the delightful lanes for eight or ten miles, in charge of one or two of the members of the committee and myself and then we returned to dinner.

"After dinner we were allowed to lounge about again and then the team were called together for football practice, a gentleman on another side of the river having placed at our disposal a suitable patch of ground. Here we worked hard for an hour and a half, perfecting ourselves in all the science of the game and mastering every trick that could be thought of. It was sport, but we were very much in earnest and though we enjoyed ourselves we spared no pains to learn everything that was to be learnt.

"Returning, we were rubbed down and examined by the trainer and then sat down to tea. After partaking of that meal we frequently took a mile and a half walk; and by ten each evening the Villa team were in bed. Such was our training day by day."

"Had you any special diet?"

"Yes. For breakfast we had ham and eggs, or fish and we drank tea or coffee. We had no lunch, except perhaps a glass of beer if we were accustomed to it. For dinner we had fish, mostly, salmon or lampreys. Not infrequently our host would bring us in a freshly-caught salmon and on one or two occasions we enjoyed ourselves by going on fishing expeditions also. Sometimes we had a little roast beef or mutton and occasionally fowl; but fish constituted dinner most frequently.

Tea consisted of chops and steaks and we went to bed without supper.

"Of course, every day was not alike and we had small adventures which formed an agreeable variation to the routine. It was our special delight to come across our fine old trainer seated by the riverside, rod in hand, waiting patiently for the fish that never came, while there was no lack of diversion at night. Pillow-fights were quite the order of the time and as most of us were used to the advantages of town life it was only natural that we should endeavour to find as much amusement as possible in that quiet out-of-the world spot. On some of the nights we were kept at the hotel entertained by the county hop-pickers out of work, who to earn an honest penny dressed themselves up like Red Indians, stuck feathers in their caps, blacked their faces and performed all sorts of wild antics, dancing and singing.

"Sometimes, too, we drove to a meet of the Worcestershire hounds at the Hundred House or Weston Park and the mention of the latter place reminds me that there Albert Brown got lost. We followed the hounds one day and most of us turned back after proceeding a mile or two. But Brown, like his immortal name-sake in America, went marching on. We missed him and could not make out where he had got to. It appeared, however, that he had walked to Droitwich, about ten miles and then started to come home. He got as far as Weston Park and could get no further. When he was ultimately rescued and restored to his sorrowing brethren he looked as if the journey had rather fatigued him.

"We were in want of nothing at Holt Fleet to make life comfortable. Our host catered for us splendidly and our friend Mr. 'Jack' Vickerstaff, who was on the committee, was in the habit of sending or bringing down some choice fish and that's the thing to train on! There were swings in front of the house and a room was set apart for boxing, while boating you may be sure we indulged in. Perhaps, take it all together, it was the happiest week of my life.

"We only had one trouble to vex our minds and that was that we had to pay a halfpenny toll every time we crossed the river. It is the only thing I can think of that was not, to our minds, as it should have been.

But even this did not overwhelm us – we bore the infliction like Britons. May no leather-chaser, now or hereafter, have more than this to vex his spirit! Well, the week ended. Some of us who were in the team may never have such a time again, but it is something to look back upon and to recall with always the same feeling of pleasure.

"When the time was up we entered upon the final matches, the Glasgow Rangers being the first to contest supremacy with us. The great struggle had to be made; the tug of war had come; and though you know how it ended perhaps it will not be uninteresting to lovers of the game to hear the story again."

Chapter 19

How We Won the Cup

"Our training being over," said Archie Hunter, "we had now the last battles to fight. On Saturday, March 5th, we met the Glasgow Rangers on neutral ground at Crewe. The Rangers had borrowed men from other first-class Scotch teams, to that we felt we were playing a representative team of Scotland and not the ordinary club, which was in itself a strong one. 'Tuck' McIntyre, brother of the famous Hugh, was the captain and among those who assisted the Rangers were Peacock, a regular 'flyer' and Forbes, who is now playing with the Blackburn Rovers.

"We had made up our minds to win and had gained so much strength after our training that we had little fear of the combination opposed to us. The ground was fairly good, but in the first half of the game we had the disadvantage of playing up a slight incline. On the whole, however, the conditions of the match were favourable to a scientific display and if it had been remarkable for nothing else it would have been remarkable for the exceptional brilliance of the play on both sides. Immense interest was taken in this match by our supporters.

"We did not travel from Holt Fleet until Saturday, going to Worcester by brake and then proceeding to Crewe without waiting at Birmingham. Our friends mustered in tremendous force and no fewer than five heavily loaded trains carrying three or four thousand of them started in the morning. One enthusiast, out of work, actually started on Friday night and walked the whole distance of fifty-four miles, determined to see the match. When he got to Crewe he met with a sympathetic friend who paid for his admittance to the ground and his fare home. This is a specimen of the burning interest which the match excited. We arrived at Crewe without mishap and found that all the arrangements for the match had been carried out excellently.

"Our opponents were a little tired with their journey, but otherwise fit and they too had 'determination in their looks' so far as we could see. In fact, the way in which they had ransacked Scotland for players was in itself a sign that they were desperately anxious to win the Cup.

"A great cheer rent the air when the teams entered the ground and this was followed by a roar of 'Play up, Villa' from the lungs of thousands of our partisans. That famous motif could also be seen on the chocolate-and-blue tickets which were worn in thousands of hats. The game began just before four o'clock, and so intense was the excitement of our followers that for a marvel they became silent and as the ball went bounding up and down the field they seemed to be holding their breaths with expectation. A little bit of neat passing, a smart run or two, one or two dangerous shots causing the goalkeepers to use their hands and then – hey presto! – I ran down the field and with the help of Brown, drove the ball through the posts within ten minutes of the start. Then you could hear the tremendous cheer with which our supporters relieved themselves and our spirits rose as we heard this jubilant and encouraging sound. But our adversaries were equally roused and exerted themselves more than ever to equalise the score. They pressed us severely and had we not played a strictly defensive game we should never have repelled the hot attack that was made upon our citadel. Almost immediately on resuming the ball was carried right into the mouth of goal and Coulton, by a somewhat indiscriminate kick, only put it in a more dangerous place. Fortunately Joey Simmonds's red-cap could be seen bobbing about where help was needed, and chiefly owing to his exertions a goal, which had appeared imminent, was saved just in the nick of time. Fiercer and fiercer became the struggle and the Rangers made a series of dashing onslaughts on our lines and if only their shooting had been less erratic the fate of the day might have been different. Presently Peacock gained the ball and sailed down with it in splendid style. He passed to Lafferty, who made a magnificent low shot which Warner was quite unable to stop and when half-time was called the game was level, one goal each being registered.

"On changing ends we had the wind in our favour and at once commenced a rattling game. Getting hold of the ball I ran down the field with it and passed to Richard Davis, who raced along with the leather at his toe, eluding the backs and the half-backs. I was close behind him and as he centred the ball beautifully across the mouth of goal I followed him up, met the leather as it came across and with a peculiar screw sent it spinning over my shoulder, completely out of the power of the goalkeeper to stop it. This caused a sensation, I can assure you and the applause which followed was simply deafening. Another goal followed and at the end we had won the fray by three goals to one. The victory was hailed with rapturous cheers and I shall never forget how elated we all were when the news reached us on the field that just at the same time the West Bromwich Albion had defeated Preston North End by the same number of goals. For now the National Cup was secured for the Midlands and whether we or the Albion actually won it was, for the moment, a very secondary matter. It was a red-letter day for us and everybody seemed to know it. We were cheered as we left the field, followed by a cheering multitude to the station and when we arrived in Birmingham we found an immense crowd assembled to welcome us.

"The Rangers took their defeat rather badly and sore disappointment was felt by their followers. But I honestly think we overplayed them altogether. Although the game was equal in the first part we felt that we had them at an advantage and in the second part the facts proved that we were much their superiors. Richard Davis and Vaughton distinguished themselves on our side and I think I may claim that this was another of my 'days out'. But let me tell you what a critic remarked at the time: 'There was little doubt,' he said, 'after the first half what the result of the struggle would be. The Rangers had not the combination that was such a conspicuous feature of the Villa play and it is scarcely surprising when the Rangers were virtually an eleven of the whole of Scotland. As a body of men they were, however, full of life and vigour and the forward division was essentially perfect. Their weakness lay in the contingent round the goal. The last half was all in favour of the Villa and fifteen minutes before the call of time it was evident that the Rangers were hopelessly beaten.

"The victory of the Albion over Preston North End was unexpected. We had fully counted upon meeting the North End in the final and it has remained one of the most startling surprises recorded in the history of football how the Albion managed to beat them. The Albion scored the two winning goals just on the call of time and doubtless their victory was due to the famous trick of their forwards' breaking away' suddenly, pressing the other side hard and unexpectedly rushing the ball through goal. This was always a great feature in the Albion's matches and one that our previous experience had prepared us for. I ought to add before turning to the next match that on returning from Crewe we were received at every station with cheers in which even the railway officials joined and at one point a signalman was observed to be making a vigorous demonstration in his lofty box. As for the final reception, it was to be remembered."

"What did the people think as to the final tie?"

"They had many doubts and could not spot the winner. Some declared without any reservation that the 'Throstles' would make rings round the Villa, others were just as certain that the Villa would utterly crush the Albion. The saving hope of Albion was said to be in Roberts, who was so much a 'stonewall' in goal as to appear to be quite unpassable. But for ourselves we still felt confident. Before playing the final tie we had a friendly contest with the Blackburn Rovers on the Leamington ground, which was covered with a four or five-inch coating of snow. The game was an exciting one and ended in a draw of three goals each. Then came the deciding match.

"At the last moment the public practically went over to the 'Throstles' and backed them heavily to win. The prophets would not prophesy good things for the Villa. The merits of the two teams were discussed and the Albion credited with superiority. It was only in our own hearts that we felt that victory would be on our own side. There had been special training for the event on both sides, of course. We had spent another week at Holt Fleet and the Albion had been to Ascot. As the time drew near the excitement manifested in the contest became more and more visible. The fact that there were two Midland teams engaged in the contest for the Blue Ribbon of the Football Field was almost too much to fully realise. Any club reaching the topmost rung of the ladder reflected honour upon the district to which it belonged, but on this occasion the Midlands had, as it were, a double lustre cast upon them. The competition was founded in 1871 and though the Cup itself is of small intrinsic value, the winning of it is a glory upon which every enthusiastic footballer sets his heart most strongly.

"The two clubs which had now to meet were old rivals and the Albion could claim to have defeated the Villa on most occasions. The Villa forwards had gained a distinction second to none in the kingdom. Summing up the claims of the players a writer said: 'The great strength in the Villa of today lies in the fact that one portion of the team does not predominate in skill or science over the other, nor can it be truthfully said that one wing of the forwards throws the other into insignificance. The backs are strong – but not abnormally so – and consequently there is little danger of the team leaving the bulk of the work to be accomplished by them. The half-backs are very strong. Burton is marvellously game, whilst the manner in which Yates tackles and screws the ball into play when it is on the verge of going out is a sight to be witnessed. Of the forwards, when all are good, it would be invidious to mark one or the other out for special distinction. The lefts, Dennis Hodgetts and Howard Vaughton, will be at a special disadvantage in having opposed to them Woodhall – certainly the finest right-wing forward in the country at the present time and the lively Tom Green. The right wing of the Villa have a somewhat easier task before them, because, though Paddock and Pearson are men of sterling merit, we fancy Albert Brown and Richard Davis are a trifle better, Davis at tackling and Brown at shooting. Of the centres, Archie Hunter and J. M. Bayliss, it can at least be said that two astuter generals it would be difficult to find. With the goalkeepers rests the key of the whole question. For many years the Albion could not find Roberts a suitable place in the field, but when at last he was fixed between the posts they then discovered what a treasure they had among them. Roberts, standing six feet one in his stockings, is a goalkeeper of whom the Albion are justly proud and if he plays as he usually does the match will rest with the 'Throstles.' Warner, the Villa custodian, is a younger hand, but the brilliant manner in which he played at Blackburn a week or two ago holds out hopes that he will do himself and his team justice. It has been stated that the Albion forwards are unscientific, but this cannot be allowed to go forth without considerable qualification.' Such was the judgement passed upon us by an impartial critic on the eve of the great contest."

the teams engaged to play in the match were as follows:-

Aston Villa: James Warner, goal; F. Coulton and J. Simmonds, backs; H. Yates, F. Dawson and J. Burton, half-backs; Albert Brown and Richard Davis, right wing; Howard Vaughton and Dennis Hodgetts, left wing; Archie Hunter, centre (captain) forwards.

West Bromwich: R. Roberts, goal; H. Green and A. T. Aldridge, backs; E. Horton, G. Timmins and C. Perry, half-backs; G. Woodhall and T. Green, right wing; T. Pearson and W. Paddock, left wing; W. Bayliss, centre (captain), forwards.

"We started for London on Friday and took up our quarters at Charterhouse Square. In the evening we had a short stroll and then retired at ten o'clock. We were up betimes in the morning, all in good spirits and happily all in good health. We met our committee and a few friends and proceeded to Kennington Oval, where presently we were joined by the members of the Albion, who were also in excellent form and very sanguine as to the result of the match. All the well-known supporters of both clubs were present in good force, including Mr. Hundly, our genial host at Holt Fleet and early in the morning heavily laden trains poured into the stations and discharged their living freight of football enthusiasts. Our chocolate-and-blue colours could be seen everywhere in the morning, especially along the Strand and all the principal thoroughfares. At half-past two there was a general stampede towards Kennington Oval and cabs, cars, carriages, traps and a thick line of pedestrians could be seen moving down the road. Arriving on the ground, it was at once manifest how great an interest the encounter had awakened. There was a dense multitude of from fifteen to twenty thousand, many familiar faces being among the number. At the last moment 5-to-4 on the Albion could be obtained and the betting in their favour was very brisk.

"A few minutes before three we entered the field and were greeted with a hearty round of cheering. I had given the Villa team special instructions how to play this match; briefly they were these – every man was to stick to his position and look after the opponent he was facing. This, of course, does not give such opportunities of brilliant play, but it is a measure of safety which I strongly commend. Let every player single out his man and determine to beat him and if he is equal to the effort the game is won. This course demands an amount of unselfishness on the part of the players which is very hard to exercise, but I have so often seen brilliance and danger combined that on such an occasion as the one I speak of we could not afford to run any such risk. Consequently the match from beginning to end was less scientific than the match with the Rangers. In this respect it was doubtless disappointing. But as a hard, fierce struggle it is not to be surpassed.

"Bayliss won the toss and I kicked off exactly at half-past three. As I did so a subdued hum of excitement could be heard and we knew that everybody's nerves were strung to the utmost. I don't know whether I am equal to describing all the details of the match. So far as play went I was cool enough, but so intent upon the game that when it was all over I could only remember a confused multitude of incidents in no particular order, but all warm, vigorous and exciting. I remember how we scampered up and down the field, what wild rushes were made, how the ball bounded here and there, the desperate charges that followed, the frenzied scrimmages, the impulsive shooting, the grand work of the goalkeepers, the attack and defence, the dangers and the relief, the terrific and prolonged struggle and yet, up to half-time, not a single goal! I recall with a thrill how we saw at one point that the Albion were getting the better of us and how we saw them with dismay closing round our citadel. Then how exhilarating it was to see the danger past, to know that the attack had been unavailing and to find ourselves racing away with the ball towards the opposite goal. How often Warner and Roberts saved I cannot tell. Time after time the shots went in scorching hot and always the men between the timbers were equal to the emergency and this was why when half the game was over there was no score.

"Changing ends, the Albion cut out the work and Hodgetts and Vaughton on our side commenced putting in an immense amount of good work. A determined attack by them was repelled by Tom Green, who got away up the field and was stopped by Coulton, who returned. From this kick Davis with a long shot centred to Hodgetts, who was close in goal and he with consummate ease, put the ball through, completely baffling Roberts. Then what a cheer arose! The Villa had scored and the jubilation of our supporters was boundless. By the time they had settled down again we were in the midst of a fast and dashing game. It seemed, however, as if no further points would be gained. Both sides were playing desperately and every man was working as if his life depended upon the victory. We were constantly in front of goal and a foul being given to the Albion there, matters looked dangerous. But it was only at the end of the game that the finishing stroke was to be given to our victory. I got possession of the ball and eluding the backs got right in front; but the ball was going at such a furious pace that I perceived I could not reach it. Roberts saw me coming and came out to meet me. Seeing the ball travelling at such a speed, I made up my mind for a desperate effort. While on the run I threw myself full length on the ground and pushed the ball with my feet past Roberts. He, in his endeavour to save, fell over me and the ball slowly went through goal before he could recover himself. This was the sensation of the day. The trick I had so successfully accomplished is not often done and it is by no means easy. You have to cast yourself down full length and throw both legs out to reach the ball and give it the necessary push. If I had not adopted this expedient I could not possibly have scored. The cheers had scarcely subsided when the whistle blew and the Villa had won the Cup by two goals to none.

"Major Marindin, President of the Football Association, who acted as referee, was good enough to say that the match was not won be science but 'by Archie Hunter's captaincy.' As soon as the whistle blew I was surrounded by the enthusiastic crowd and for a few moments I thought I should be torn in pieces. They nearly wrung my hand off and those who could not get near enough put all the heart they could into shouting 'Bravo, Archie' and 'Well done, Villa.' Finally, I was lifted shoulder-high and amid the wildest demonstrations carried all round the field, nor would my zealous friends release me until the moment came when I was called upon to receive the Cup.

"The pavilion in which the ceremony took place was thronged and amongst the company were many ladies. Major Marindin made the presentation. He said the Cup was not so much to be valued for its intrinsic worth as for the honour it conferred upon those who possessed it. Aston Villa deserved the trophy, but a word of sympathy was due to the 'runners-up,' the West Bromwich Albion. A report of the proceedings stated that when I was presented with the treasured trophy I was 'beaming through the blotches of dirt which besmeared my face.' I daresay I was. I certainly felt very proud and happy, as we all did, when the gold medals were next given to us by Miss Marindin.

"The news of our victory was received in Birmingham, as might have been expected, with indescribable delight. As for the Albion, they took defeat rather sorely and their supporters were terribly chagrined. A report was current that many of the Black Country people had sold their pigs and their household goods to back them and that the reverse so far affected them that they were obliged to go without their Sunday's dinner. On Monday the shutters were up at many of the shops as a sign of mourning and for a whole week the consternation and despair were manifest. The team arrived at West Bromwich at four o'clock on Sunday morning and found the station deserted. It had been originally arranged that we should return on the Monday, but at the last moment our plans were changed and we left London at midnight. At half-past three in the morning, just twelve hours after the great game had begun, we arrived at New Street Station and what a sight met our eyes!

"The huge platforms were crowded and as the train steamed into the station a band struck up the jubilant strains of 'See The Conquering Hero Comes.' We could scarcely get out of the carriage for the crowd that surged round and the deafening cheers which resounded through the station produced a sensation which will never be forgotten by any of us. The enthusiastic multitude followed me home and early the next morning were trooping round again and inquiring for me.

"The Bell Inn, where I resided, had been illuminated and all Saturday night the street was blocked. At half-past twelve on Sunday the house was too small to hold the crowd who came and demanded admission and the reception I had was something to remember all my life. Mr. Powell, the proprietor of the Bell, drove over to Mr. Kynoch's, our President and returned with the English Cup.

"Congratulations showered upon us from all quarters and our year of jubilee finished with this crowning triumph. The match with the Albion was the fiftieth we had played, so that 1887 was a year of jubilee to the Villa in more senses than one and made a record which has not to the present been exceeded."

Chapter 20

Conclusion

"And now," said Archie Hunter, "I will briefly sum up the most important events in the Aston Villa Club so far as I was actively connected with them. We had two excellent seasons after the winning of the English Cup and our hopes were high that we might be able to win the trophy again.

"The fight for the Championship was in each case a prolonged struggle from which we emerged with some of the honours of war, although we were not finally successful. In the 1887-8 season we were left to fight Preston North End. Let me tell you as succinctly as I can the curious history of that encounter and its unexpected sequel. As usual, we went into training in our old quarters and Preston North End also made special arrangements. At the end of our week at Holt Fleet we left amid the lusty cheers of the inhabitants and many friends who had assembled to wish us a repetition of the previous year's success. Arriving in Birmingham, we dined in charge of Dr. Jones and then drove in a coach to Perry Barr. Scarcely had we started upon the road than we were surprised at the huge concourse wending their way down towards our ground and when we got on the main road the scene was simply like a Derby day. An endless line of vehicles could be seen slowly moving down and an empty string of vehicles returning; so we had to take our place behind the rest and quietly move along in turn with the rest.

"We were soon recognised and amid the exciting hubbub could be heard the encouraging and familiar shout of 'Play up, Villa,' while others singled me out and cheered me all along the way. No one could tell, however, exactly what the fortune of the day would be; certainly no one was prepared for what actually occurred. Preston North End was captained by Nick Ross and the team was much the same as we had met before. The contest between the North End and ourselves had always been keen and everyone anticipated a close match.

"Our committee had made tremendous exertions, perhaps almost unparalleled, to secure the convenience of spectators and players. They had gone so far as to ask the local police superintendent to send mounted constables to preserve the field from invasion and to guarantee that the match should be played out without hindrance. The Superintendent said that he would have a sufficient force for our purpose, but he must have under-estimated the crowd. The crowd was, in fact, a source of amazement to us all. Half-a-crown or more was paid willingly for the slightest coign of vantage; trees were climbed, roofs invaded and one enthusiast gallantly perched himself upon the flag-pole, where, I think, he was as well off as anybody.

"An hour before the game was announced to commence it seemed impossible to crush any more on to the ground; yet the stream still rolled on and at length the barriers gave way. The forty police were unable to check the rush that followed and Mr. Ramsay at once telegraphed for the Hussars. It was difficult for the officials to prevent the spectators from spreading over the meadow and though the crowd was well behaved, yet their presence on the field had a disturbing effect. Well, having kept them beyond the touch-lines, the two teams emerged from the tent to do battle.

"We went on the field amid a storm of cheers, never suspecting that we should be interfered with. Scarcely ten minutes had passed when the game thoroughly warmed up and I received the ball from Allen, shot along with it between the two opposition backs and scored the first goal. It was done so quickly that I well remember the look of surprise and consternation on the faces of the Preston team when they realised all that had happened. But a great shout of jubilation rent the air when the same fact was realised by the spectators and cries of 'Well done, Archie' and 'The Villa wins' could be heard from all parts. A few minutes afterwards, while we were playing a very strong game and had the upper hand of our opponents, we made another attack upon the Preston goal and Tom Green, who was notorious, among other things, for being off-side, played the ball when in a position to score a second time. An appeal for off-side followed and to the great disappointment of all, though the decision was perfectly just, judgement was given against us.

"But while this had been going on the crowd had gradually drawn closer and got altogether beyond bounds. They were swarming over the meadow and further play was impossible. The people were breaking through the barriers and those at the back were pushing forward those at the front and encroaching upon the playing ground. The Preston team gathered in a group and sat on the ground while our players were told to assist the police in clearing the lines. I myself, having some influence with the populace in those days, was particularly requested to speak to the people and induce them to return to their places. I went forward and begged of them to withdraw, pointing out that there was an empty space of a dozen yards or more at the back. But they would not be reasoned with and I next tried to push the multitude back, with the help of a posse of police and I never worked so hard and so ineffectually in my life. I might as well have tried to move a mountain. All my efforts were unavailing. Two Hussars upon the ground mounted cab horses and careered round as wildly as their dashing steeds would allow them and this did some good. The people retreated a little and we proposed to continue the game. But first, a consultation took place between the two captains, the umpires and the referee and taking into consideration the fact that the game might again be interrupted, both captains agreed that it should be no Cup tie.

"We started again on the full understanding that a friendly game was to be played so as not to disappoint the spectators. But this fact had a depressing effect upon the Villa players; they would not exert themselves and we lost the game by three goals to one. It was a welcome relief to us all when the whistle sounded, for the crowd had again grown unruly and the mounted police arrived too late to be of any use.

"Well, I have now to tell you the strange conclusion to this curious episode. The reports of the umpires and the referee were received by the Association and discussed at their meeting at Kennington Oval. But what was our amazement and consternation to find that Preston North End was claiming to have won the match! Considering the definite agreement come to on the field this was startling and we were not prepared for it. A vote was taken whether the match should be played again or not and an equal number was recorded on both sides. Major Marindin then gave his casting vote in favour of Preston North End, blaming Aston Villa for not having made proper provision for the match. I have no great desire to re-open the question now and it has been bitterly discussed on both sides. But I should like to say this: that if fault there were at all it was not on the part of our committee, but on the part of the police superintendent, who declared that he had made sufficient preparations and then left us in the lurch.

"This then, is how we lost the Cup in 1888 and you will understand how keen our disappointment was in losing under such circumstances. We had another try for the trophy the following season and met the Blackburn Rovers in the final. On this occasion we trained at Great Haywood, Cannock Chase, a place which was specially recommended to us by one of our supporters. Here a series of misfortunes overtook us. On our arrival we strolled out and as I was walking along the road with a member of the committee, the night being pitch dark, I caught my toe in a grating, overbalanced myself and so severely injured my foot that gout ensued and I was incapacitated for the rest of the week. Instead of joining in the exercise day by day I was sitting in the hostelry with my leg stretched up and not even able to wear a shoe.

"Here was a nice predicament for a man who had to play in a Cup tie on Saturday! Not only was I suffering myself, but I was unable to devote any attention to the team and Tom Green, who also had to play, was laid up all the week with a bad toe which had been injured in a match. These disasters had their effect. We were rather dispirited and when the match was played few of us were in our usual form and the Rovers inflicted upon us a severe defeat.

"This was the last English Cup tie in which I took part and though I did not know it then, my career as a footballer was rapidly coming to an end. I broke down while playing Everton the following season. The ground was in a fearful condition after heavy rain. Pools of water and masses of mud made play almost impossible and to add to our troubles a biting east wind was cutting us and seemed to pierce us like a knife. I was playing my hardest when I fell into a pool of water. Just before I had received a severe bruise and with the additional shock to the system I fainted away. On reaching home I was advised to relinquish play and that advice I have taken.

"There are no more Triumphs of the Football Field for me. I have thrown in my lot with the Committee and shall do all I can to foster the game. But often, when acting as umpire for my old team, I have been almost carried away with the excitement of the game and would have given anything to rush to my old position, get the ball at my toe and race with it down the field. And whenever the leather comes bounding by me it is hard to resist passing it on to one of my old colleagues playing around me. I can't tell you how sorry I am to be out of the game henceforward; but I have had my day and must be satisfied."

"What do you consider the best of your feats, Mr. Hunter?"

"The best thing a forward can do is to dribble the ball through all opposition and score. This I have done many times; in fact, 'Archie's runs' were sufficiently frequent to obtain a sort of celebrity. I was particularly fortunate in my play when my brother Andy was my partner. He was so accurate and so reliable that I was able to put forth my best efforts and make certain of getting the ball through goal. A forward to be worth anything must be a complete master of the dribbling game, must have good judgement and be sufficiently strong to resist the charges and bumps of his opponents."

"Which do you consider the best match you ever played in?"

"That is very difficult to say, matches vary so in character and yet may be equally good. I think when we played Queen's Park in a storm and scored five goals with amazing speed that the Villa were seen at their best, especially as Queen's Park were considered well nigh invincible then. Again, our draw with West Bromwich Albion, three goals each, was a magnificent game. Mr. Hinks, our President, wrote a letter to the committee congratulating Albert Brown and myself upon our play and there was not a man on either side but deserved praised. The struggle was one of the finest ever seen in the Midlands and perhaps one of the finest ever seen in the kingdom."

"I suppose you have often met with exciting incidents, Mr. Hunter?"

"Well, in its way, every match is an exciting incident more or less," Archie replied. "But it was awfully exciting for us and for the spectators when we played Darwen and up to half-time had all the advantage, while in the second half they scored rapidly and it was only at the last minute that we pulled the game out of the fire. Another exciting incident was when, in the earlier part of our history, the Villa were drawn against two teams on one day and we were obliged to use our second set to play a first team match. I was chosen to captain the second team against Elwell's and the first team went to Newport, under the captaincy of my brother Andy. The result of the two matches was sensational. Here was our first team, with one or two of the best men missing, pitted against a powerful team playing its full strength and Andy led our men to victory, scoring six goals to none. Then there was our second team pitted against a first team in good condition and we were victorious after a most desperate struggle, only scoring the winning goal just as the whistle was blown. It was this double triumph of the Villa which had so stimulating an effect upon the players and rapidly advanced its fortune."

"Do you often find the game amusing in any way?"

"No, it is on the whole a very serious game. Sometimes the antics of an individual player will cause a little hilarity, as in the case of 'little Roberts,' the Welshman in our team, but the play is too exciting for fun. It used to be very amusing at one time, before a rule was made stopping the practice as dangerous, to see the backs fall down in the field and cause their opponents to fly headlong over them, sometimes yards away. I have done the trick many times. You see your opponent advancing at top speed with the ball and instead of trying to take the leather from him you drop suddenly upon your knee and over he goes, probably falling heavily on his shoulder. Of course it was highly dangerous and a man might have broken his neck and thus a rule was properly passed prohibiting it."

"What is your opinion of the game at present, Mr. Hunter?"

"I am convinced that it will maintain its position as the most popular game in this country and that it will remain at the head of scientific sports. There is one enthusiasm for cricket and another for football and the enthusiasm for the latter game appears to me to be excited by deeper and heartier feelings. At all events I have no fear that football will decline, though I am sorry that it is so largely maintained by the professional element. Speaking as a professional myself, I may say that I can only look upon professionalism as an unavoidable misfortune. While it is of immense assistance to the game in many respects, it appears to me that it lowers its character and I myself should have felt happier very often if I could have continued to play as an amateur and so regarded the game as a game and not as a business. However, this is a matter for the Association to deal with.

"I should like, as one who has been credited with some success in dealing with a football team, to offer a little advice to captains – to those who are not accustomed to their duties yet, or who may be called upon at some future time to assume the position. First and foremost I would impress this upon them – treat the players as men and not as schoolboys. I have seen a great deal of mischief resulting from neglect to do this. When the players are only treated as boys they are apt to regard themselves as boys and act accordingly. They become selfish, obstinate and quarrelsome, turn sulky if they are displeased, or wrangle with one another on the field. Insubordination can never be provided against unless every player is made to feel that he will be called to account as a man and I am certain that this system works well.

"Then let all prejudices be avoided. I have known Scotchmen or Welshmen disliked by Englishmen simply on account of their nationality and I have known Scotchmen and Welshmen act just in the same way towards Englishmen. Now these prejudices ought to be stamped out. The team, however it is composed, must play as a team and not as a gathering of different men out of harmony with each other. I always tried to foster good feeling in Aston Villa and I think we were one of the merriest and happiest teams in the country. For myself I never bothered my head about the country a man came from and as long as we had good players and good fellows among us, it mattered not whether they were English, Scotch or Welsh.

"As to guiding the players, I think a captain should make it one of the first rules that every man should get into the habit of defending his position. I greatly dislike to see men scampering wildly over the field, leaving their places unprotected, forgetting their own particular duty and doing another man's work. If a man is playing back let him remember that and single out his opponent and be prepared to tackle him whenever the opportunity arises. We won the match with the West Bromwich Albion through sticking to this plan and I think many more matches would be more evenly contested if the custom were more generally adopted.

"The greatest mistake which players are in the habit of making and one which I most often cautioned my team about, is this: when they think there is a foul, or that somebody has played off-side, they stop dead in their play and wait for the referee's decision. This has lost many a match that should have been won. Young players especially cannot be told too often that it is not they who can stop the game and however sure they may be that an appeal will be supported, they must on no account relax their efforts until the whistle sounds. I have seen many times, at a doubtful point in the game, the ball rushed through goal simply because no opposition has been offered and then, perhaps, the referee has decided that the game ought to have been continued and allowed the goal. Most clubs have suffered in this way and I would earnestly impress upon footballers the necessity of playing their hardest until a definite order is given to them to cease.

"And now," said Archie, "I must bring these remarks to an end. It has been pleasant to me to recall the varying fortune of the club to which I am so closely attached and which has provided me with some of the most enjoyable days of sport that I have ever had. I must again say how sorry I am that I am no longer the captain of Aston Villa, but all that I can do for its future success – and we hope next year to bring it to the front rank again – I shall do heartily.

"Let me also place on record my appreciation of the loyalty and goodwill which I experienced from all the members of the team during my captaincy and at the same time I should like to express the deep gratification I feel that my football career helped me to make so many good and steadfast friends all over the kingdom. Glancing back, I can see a multitude of famous players who have helped me to spend many a pleasant hour and who always have a welcome for me when I meet them in other walks of life. After all, I should admire football if it were only for the fact that it brings a number of manly, spirited and gallant players into association with one another and promotes good-fellowship which seldom knows any diminution."

With these words Archie Hunter wished me good-bye and thus brought his last interview to a close.

Other Aston Villa titles published by Sports Projects Ltd

VILLA PARK • 100 YEARS

SIMON INGLIS – £24.95

A celebration of the centenary of one of the world's finest stadiums.

240 pages... hardback... large A4 format... printed full colour... colour dustjacket... over 200 illustrations.

ISBN 0-946866-43-0

STRIDE INSIDE THE VILLA

STEVE STRIDE (WITH ROB BISHOP) – £8.95

Club Secretary and Director Steve Stride tells his story of 25 years at Villa Park.

160 pages... hardback... A5 format... printed mono... colour dustjacket.

ISBN 0-946866-40-6

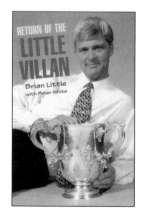

RETURN OF THE LITTLE VILLAN

BRIAN LITTLE (WITH PETER WHITE) – £11.95

The Manager's account of his first 20 months in charge of the club he joined as an apprentice.

184 pages... hardback... large A5 format... printed mono with colour picture section... colour dustjacket.

ISBN 0-946866-35-X